MODERN JAZZ GUITAR TECHNIQUE

by *Adrian Ingram,* F.L.C.M., L.T.C.L., (T.D.), A.L.C.M., Cert.Ed.

Copyright © 1980

NORTHAMPTON GUITAR STUDIOS
Music Publishers
46 Brookland Road, Northampton, England

International Standard Book Number ISBN 0 9506949 0 8

World Copyright.   Made in Great Britain

All rights reserved, including the right of reproduction in whole or in part
in any form or by any means without the prior permission
of the copyright owners.

Cover Design and Illustrations by William Oliver Ford

Phototypesetting by Time Graphics (Northampton) Limited

Printed by G. B. Rotorgraph Limited, Northampton

Published and Distributed by

NORTHAMPTON GUITAR STUDIOS, Music Publishers
46 Brookland Road, Northampton, England

£5.50

Adrian Ingram

Adrian Ingram was born in Birmingham in 1950 and at the age of nine began playing the guitar. Several years later he became deeply interested in modern jazz after hearing Wes Montgomery. Since becoming a professional player his demands as a guitarist have taken him on European tours, accompanying famous American artistes, undertaking session work, and playing for records, radio and television.

In 1972 Adrian Ingram trained professionally as a music teacher and classical guitarist and, on completion of his training obtained a Fellowship of the London College of Music. (The highest diploma awarded for guitar performance). Since returning to his first love, jazz, Adrian has been contributing extensively to jazz education by establishing jazz workshops at Birmingham and Manchester and he has become internationally well known by his series of jazz guitar articles in leading guitar magazines. At the invitation of Birmingham University Adrian Ingram will be giving lectures on Jazz History.

Adrian's vast experience of Jazz and Classical music coupled with his many playing activities and high qualifications as a guitar teacher have been instrumental in making this publication, "MODERN JAZZ GUITAR TECHNIQUE", the finest and most comprehensive jazz guitar course of its kind.

Guitarists of all standards and abilities and non-jazz musicians too will enrich their playing and knowledge by the wealth of information and practical guidance contained within these covers.

Adrian Ingram is an outstanding guitarist, musician and teacher and this book fills an important gap in Modern Jazz education.

RICHARD J. COBBY, 1980
Northampton, England.

CONTENTS

INTRODUCTION

As this course is aimed primarily at the guitarist who wishes to learn more about the mysteries of jazz guitar playing, I am basing many of the ideas upon the jazz guitar styles of the late nineteen-forties and early nineteen-fifties. My reason for choosing this particular era in the development of the jazz guitar is that the guitar pioneers of this period: Tal Farlow, Barney Kessel, Johnny Smith, Chuck Wayne, Charlie Christian, Sal Salvador, Billy Bauer, Jimmy Raney and many, many more have in some way or another influenced the new generation of jazz guitarists many of whom, including such important figures as George Benson, Pat Martino and Larry Coryell, openly acknowledge their debt to these masters.

The course is set out in three parts, theoretical, practical chord work and solo playing dealing with linear improvisation. Each section may be worked independently depending upon the guitarists particular needs. The theoretical section was conceived to provide an insight into jazz chord construction and application, outlining the basic principles of modern harmony and tonality. This is followed by the theory of improvisation as derived from basic scales and modes. Whilst the practical sections are concerned solely with the development of guitar technique which may be used as a foundation for your own guitar improvisations in a modern jazz idiom.

ADRIAN INGRAM, 1980

ACKNOWLEDGEMENTS

Photograph Credits – The Author and Publishers wish to thank the following:

Page 23: Herb Ellis — courtesy of Ashley Summerfield.

Page 24: Ike Isaacs with Wes Montgomery photograph G. Clinton used by permission of I. Isaacs.

Page 25: Joe Pass — Pablo Records, courtesy of Maurice Summerfield.

Page 29: Django Reinhardt courtesy of Maurice Summerfield.

Page 31: Charlie Byrd, Barney Kessel and Herb Ellis — Walkerprint.

Page 38: Barney Kessel — Robert Martin, Stockholm, Sweden, courtesy of Big Bear Records.

Page 79: Charles Mingus — photograph WEA/Honorarfrei courtesy of Jazz Journal.

Despite research, we have been unable to locate the copyright owners of several photographs used and of solo extracts transcribed from recordings. Therefore, we have proceeded on the assumption that there is no formal copyright on the music and that the photographs are publicity pictures. If we have inadvertently published previously copyrighted material without proper permission, we advise the owner of that copyright to contact us so that the appropriate acknowledgement may be given in future editions.

Northampton Guitar Studios, Music Publishers.

THEORY

SECTION 1 (Theoretical)

THE FUNDAMENTALS OF MODERN HARMONY

Many guitar students are at once puzzled by the term *harmony*. The particular jargon connected with the word, including other such peculiar words as 'root, triad, dominant, dissonance' often prove too much in themselves for the student to negotiate. As a result frustration sets in and the study of harmony is abandoned even before the subject is allowed to become remotely interesting.

One of the main characteristics of modern jazz harmony is the use of extra notes added to a basic chord, the 6th, 7th, 9th, 11th and 13th degrees of a major scale, whilst the ♭5th almost became an obsession, especially during the late nineteen-forties.

Compare the following Chords. The first is a ♭5th chord, the second a straight-forward major chord.

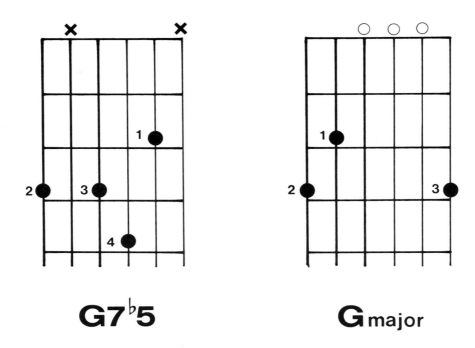

Listen carefully to the dissonance produced by the ♭5th chord. Try using this chord yourself at the end of a tune in the place of an ordinary major chord and you will experience the well-loved bop *cliche* for yourself.

Now that you know what a ♭5th chord sounds like, you may like to know exactly what the term ♭5th means.

To fully understand what is meant by 6th, 7th, 13th, ♭5th etc., it is necessary to have a working knowledge of **intervals.**

INTERVALS

A musical interval is the difference in pitch between two notes sounded either simultaneously or consecutively. Two notes played consecutively form what is known as a melodic interval, whilst two notes played together form a harmonic interval.

The major scale is always used to work out the name of a particular interval. The lines and spaces between the two notes are counted as such:

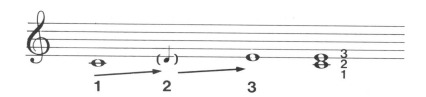

There are three notes between C and E (c, d, e) therefore the interval is a 3rd.

Major 2nd	Major 3rd	Perfect 4th	Perfect 5th	Major 6th	Major 7th	Octave

Either of the notes forming an interval may be sharpened or flattened. Try to learn the following principles.

1. A flattened major interval becomes a minor one.

Maj 3rd   **Min 3rd**   **Min 3rd**

major 3rd becomes a minor 3rd which could also be written

2. Flattened 3rds and 7ths (minor intervals) can be flattened once more to become diminished intervals, represented in popular music by the sign ° or the word dim.

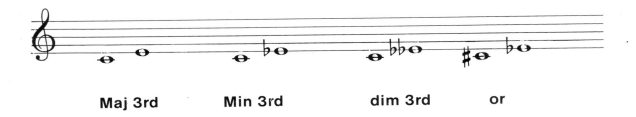

Maj 3rd   **Min 3rd**   **dim 3rd**   **or**

3. Perfect intervals (4th, 5th and octave) can be flattened only once to become diminished.

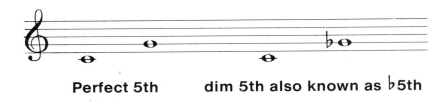

Perfect 5th   **dim 5th also known as ♭5th**

4. All perfect intervals and the major 6th and 7th can be sharpened to become augmented intervals (represented by **+** and 'aug').

Perfect 5th   **aug 5th**   **or**

5. Intervals greater than the octave (8th) are called compound intervals and these are used very frequently in jazz.

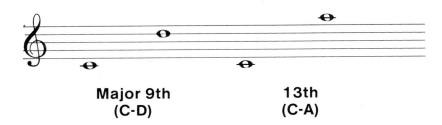

Major 9th   **13th**
(C-D)   **(C-A)**

THE THEORY OF CHORD CONSTRUCTION

A chord is produced whenever three or more notes are sounded together and the word **triad** simply means a three note chord.

A basic triad consists of a root note, which can be any note of the scale, with the intervals of a 3rd and a 5th added above it.

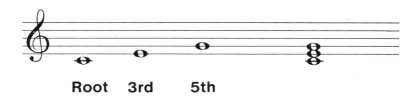

Root   3rd   5th

A triad can be made from every note of the scale. The quickest way to harmonize a note by completing the basic triad is to fill in the two lines or spaces directly above that note.

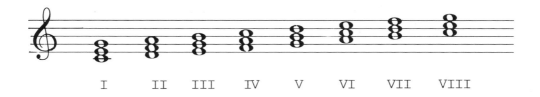

I   II   III   IV   V   VI   VII   VIII

A fully harmonized C major scale looks like this:

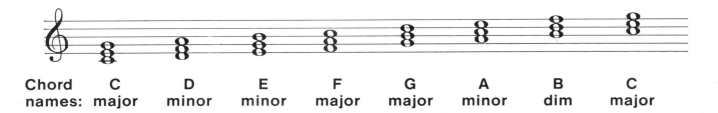

Chord names:	C major	D minor	E minor	F major	G major	A minor	B dim	C major

Now that you know what is meant by the use of figures such as 6th, ♭5 and 9th, and how a basic triad is formed we will look at the principle of altered chords.

An ordinary major chord as we have seen consists of the root and a third and a 5th and any alteration or additional note is indicated by a qualifying symbol such as m, m6, m9, etc.

Here are some examples of an altered C chord:

C   is the root plus 3rd and 5th above.

Cm   root, ♭3 and 5th.

C6   an ordinary C triad with an added major 6th.

Cm6   is the triad of Cm with an added major 6th.

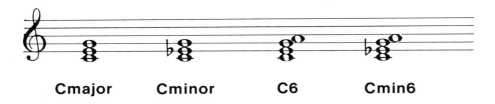

Cmajor   **Cminor**   **C6**   **Cmin6**

Notes altered or added: ♭3,   6th (A)   ♭3 and added 6(A)

Chords based on a major triad with an added ♭7 (minor 7th):

C7 is the chord of C major with an added minor 7th.

C7 the B♭ note is the ♭7th.

C9 is the basic C major triad plus the ♭7th and a major 9th.

C9 the 9th note is the D.

C11   the basic C triad plus the ♭7th and the major 11th note (sometimes a 9th is included).

C11   the F being the added 11th note.

C13 The basic C triad plus ♭7th and major 13th (sometimes the 9th and
      11th are also added).

C13 The added 13th
being the high A.

To form the minor inversions of these chords Cm7, Cm9, Cm11, Cm13, the
procedure is the same, but remember that the basic triad must now be
minor and therefore must include the ♭3rd note.

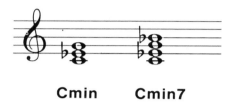

Cmin   **Cmin7**

Now that you have seen how we arrive at these altered jazz chords you
should be able to grasp the following:

C aug (+)   **basic major triad plus ♯5th.**

C7 + 5   **Basic major triad with ♭7th and ♯5th.**

C7dim5   **basic major triad with ♭7th and ♭5th.**

Cmaj7   **the basic C major triad with an added 7th (major).**

Csus4   **Basic C major triad plus an added major 4th (sometimes
                 the major 3rd is omitted or delayed in this chord).**

Csus4 its use is generally to decorate a major triad by delaying the
       appearance of the 3rd, the 4th often being a suspended note from
       the previous chord.

In the practical application of these chords you will find that often one or more of the notes will be omitted.

Note also that on the guitar the basic triad is often padded out to give a fuller sound by the doubling of one or more of its constituent notes, for example a basic

G major triad   is often played:

THE "VOICING" OF CHORDS

As there are three notes in the basic triad, there are three ways to play it.

1. The root position, which has the root in the bass:

2. The first inversion, which has the 3rd of the chord in the bass:

3. The second inversion, which has the 5th of the chord in the bass.

Each time that we add another note to a triad we extend the possibilities for inversion. For example the 7th chord is capable of four inversions:

You can of course also raise or lower these chords an octave. Each of these different ways of playing the same chord is known as a chord *"voicing"*.

AMBIGUOUS CHORDS

It is this inverting or voicing of a chord that leads to many confusing ambiguities. The fact that a triad may be played in three different ways also means that it can be given three different names! This accounts for the question that many students find themselves asking, "Why can the same chord have more than one name?"

To try to explain this particular problem, look at the following:

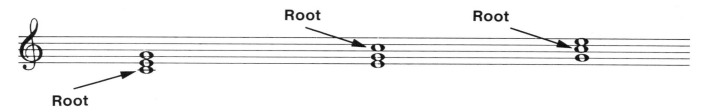

Okay at first appearance we have three C major chords, a root chord with a C in the bass, a first inversion with an E in the bass and a second inversion with a G in the bass, but there are other ways of viewing these chords.

Let us look again at these three chords ignoring their relationship to the key of C major. What do we have for instance if we treat each bass note as the root of the chord?

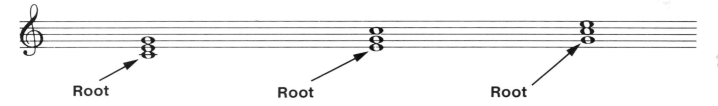

The first chord would be a C major as before, but the second chord would be Emb6 and the third chord would be G6 with an added 4th!

The ambiguity continues if we decide to call the second note of each chord the root note and so it goes on. To make matters even more complicated, sometimes an imaginary root is used, i.e. a note that is not even included in the chord, for example:

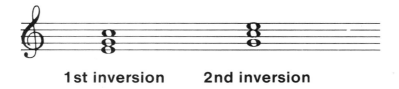

1st inversion   2nd inversion

the 1st and 2nd inversion of a C major chord could also be thought of as:

Ami7, if we use A as an imaginary root.

TECHNICAL NAMES FOR THE NOTES OF THE SCALE

These are very useful to know but they are by no means essential to the art of jazz. Certain terms such tonic, sub-dominant, dominant and dominant seventh are however used quite frequently by musicians and it is as well for the guitarist to understand their meaning.

Besides numbering our scale I - VIII we can also give each note a special name.

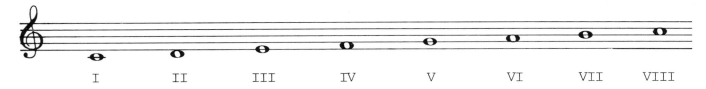

| I | II | III | IV | V | VI | VII | VIII |

can also be:

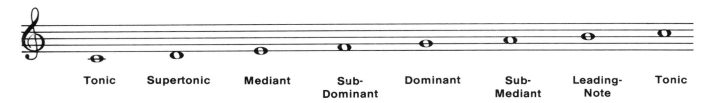

| Tonic | Supertonic | Mediant | Sub-Dominant | Dominant | Sub-Mediant | Leading-Note | Tonic |

The word dominant 7th means the dominant chord with an added minor 7th note.

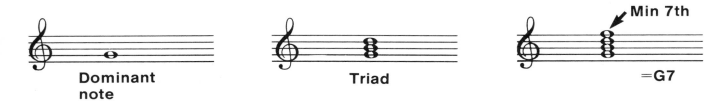

Dominant note   **Triad**   **Min 7th**   **=G7**

is the dominant 7th chord in the key of C major, the F note being the added minor 7th, while the basic triad is formed on the dominant note (V (G)) of the C scale.

For practice in the quick recognition of these words work out the following exercises on paper:

EXAMPLE:

1. Tonic, mediant, dominant, dom7th, tonic is C Major would be:

    I III V V7 I

    or

    C Em G G7 C

Now work out the following for yourself:

1. Sub-dominant, mediant, dom7th, tonic, in F Major.

2. Tonic, sub-dom, dominant, tonic, in B♭ Major.

3. **Tonic, sub-mediant, dom7th, tonic, in C Major.**

4. **Tonic, mediant, sub-mediant, dominant, dom7th, tonic, in G Major.**

These names also apply to the minor scale.

SUBSTITUTE CHORDS

Many chord sequences can be improved by the use of substitute chords — however experience and good taste is needed for successful substitution and care must be taken to ensure that the substitution fits the melody notes.

The main reasons for using substitute chords are:

A   To create tension.

B   To create an element of surprise.

C   To extend the possibilities for melodic improvisation.

D   To strengthen a weak or an uninteresting progression.

To help you to acquire some experience in the art of chord substitution I have listed some of the common substitutions. These should serve as an introduction to the art. There are of course infinite possibilities and eventually good taste and your ears will be your best guide.

The art of chord substitution does not really depend on any particular fundamental rule, formula or principle and jazz musicians often use very remote and unpredictable substitute chords, the acid test is really, how effectively the musician **resolves** his chord or chords.

Substitutions in popular use:

I   **substitute any of: I7 I9 IIIm7 I13 VI7**

V or V7   substitute any from: V9 V13 V7♭5 II7

IV   substitute any of: IV9 IV7 IV13 ♭VII7

CHORD SUPERIMPOSITION

This is the changing of the basic chord to a chord with the same root name i.e., C9 in place of C7. Although this is generally classed as chord substitution it is not really substitution in a strict sense, in that often the basic chord remains the same.

The most common chords using this device are 9th, 13th and 11th all of which are produced by superimposing intervals of a third above the 7th chord, adding colour and texture without sacrificing the effect of the basic tonality.

This idea is illustrated in the earlier section 'the theory of chord construction'.

It must be remembered that the extension of the 7th chord offers many harmonic possibilities and a much greater scope for improvisation. Charlie Parker once stated that much of his style was created from the use of extended chords, or as he called them 'the upper partials of a chord'.

Basic superimpositions are:

9th, ♭9th, +9th, 11th, +11th, 13th.

IMPROVISATION ON RELATED SCALES

For every chord there is a related scale from which notes may be used when improvising. Therefore a guitarist can play any of the notes from this related scale against the chord and none will sound musically wrong, though some combinations will sound more effective than others.

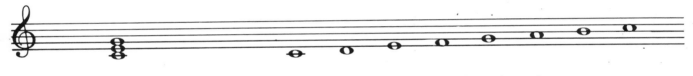

C major Chord   **C major related scale**

If you can get another guitarist to play a C major chord, try playing the notes of the related scale in any order or rhythm against it.

Here are a few examples:

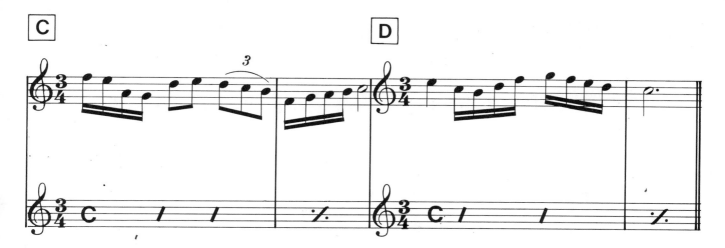

None of these examples sounds out of tune, and if you keep to the related scale, none of your own improvisations will sound out of tune. This method of composing on the spot, generally known as improvisation, is fundamental to the art form, and as mentioned earlier some combinations of notes will sound better than others. The choice of note arrangement depends on the experience, the ingenuity and the basic style of the performer. There are obviously countless possibilities both rhythmic and melodic and I strongly suggest that you listen to as much jazz music as you can to assimilate ideas.

THE C MINOR CHORD AND IT'S RELATED SCALES

There are two related minor scales, the harmonic minor and the melodic minor.

The harmonic scale has its 3rd and 6th notes flattened.

OR

The other minor scale (melodic) uses different notes ascending and descending, and is not so popular as the harmonic scale for improvisation, though combinations of the two are often employed.

OR

Note that the melodic minor scale uses a sharpened 6th and 7th note when ascending, but restores these notes when descending.

Again experiment with these related scales by playing them over a C minor chord, trying various rhythmic and melodic combinations.

The related major and minor scales are written here in the key of C for ease of reference. It is essential that you transpose them into other keys and this should present no real difficulty for the new keynote is also the first note of the new related scale.

DOMINANT 7th RELATED SCALES

The dominant 7th chord uses it's tonic as a related scale for example:

C7 uses the scale of F, C7 being the dominant 7th chord in the key of F.

G7 uses the scale of C.

D7 uses the scale of G.

If you find these difficult to work out, the following table will prove useful:

CHORD	USES	SCALE
C7	—	F
G7	—	C
D7	—	G
A7	—	D
E7	—	A
B7	—	E
F♯7	—	B
C♯7	—	F♯
G♯7	—	C♯
F7	—	B♭
B♭7	—	E♭
E♭7	—	A♭
A♭7	—	D♭
D♭7	—	G♭
G♭7	—	C♭

DIMINISHED RELATED SCALES

Because of its ambiguous nature the diminished chord uses a special scale built from a tone and a semitone alternating:

There are three basic diminished scales which, like the chords, when inverted repeat themselves over and over again.

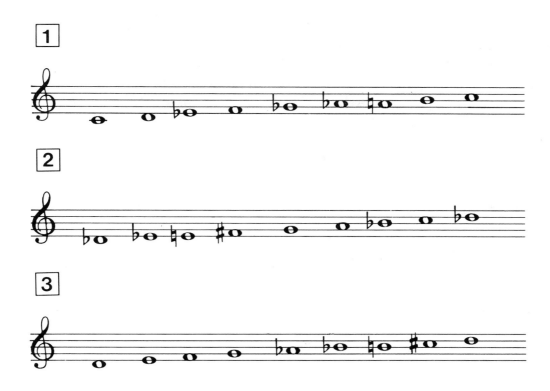

SCALE 1 May be used for: Cdim, E♭dim, F♯dim, Adim.

SCALE 2 May be used for: C♯dim, Edim, Gdim, B♭dim.

SCALE 3 May be used for: Ddim, Fdim, A♭dim, Bdim.

They can also be used (as the related scales) to minor 7th and minor 6th chords.

AUGMENTED RELATED SCALES

The scale that is used for improvisation over an augmented chord is the whole tone. This scale contains the notes of a basic augmented triad, and may be used freely against any augmented chord.

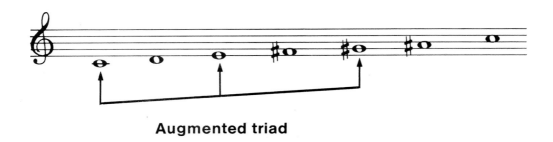

Augmented triad

As there are only four basic augmented chords C, C♯, D and E (all others being inversions of these) it is essential to memorize which scales go with which chord.

Matters are simplified by the fact that there are only two augmented scales C and C♯.

C

C♯

Note that some of the notes in these two scales are often enharmonically changed, i.e.,

C   **C♯**

Because each note of this scale is a tone (two frets) apart, it is often referred to as the Whole Tone scale. These scales may be played at any pitch and can be inverted so that a new scale may be constructed from each of its notes.

The seven inversions of the C whole tone scale.

20

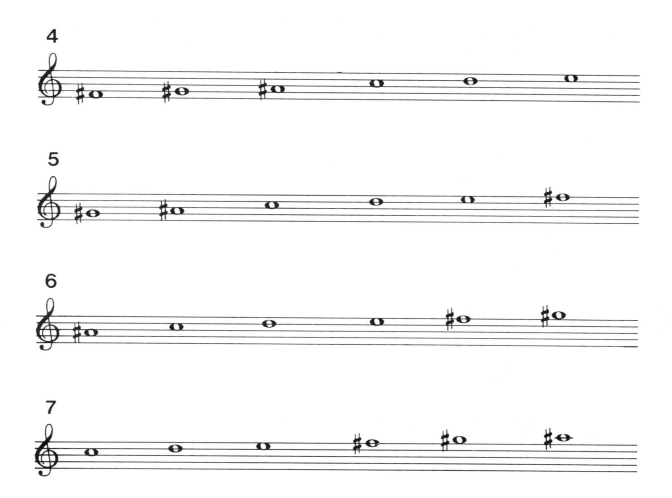

Memorize the following table:

The whole tone scale beginning on C can be used against:
Caug, Daug, Eaug, Faug, Gaug, A♭aug and B♭aug.

The whole tone scale beginning on C♯ can be used against:
C♯aug, E♭aug, Faug, Gaug, Aaug, and Baug.

EXAMPLES OF IMPROVISION USING RELATED SCALES

Django Reinhardt

This improvised passage from 'Dinah' by Django Reinhardt uses the related scale of G Major against a G chord and this scale is then continued to become the related scale of D7.

Mundell Lowe

This passage begins the tune 'After You've Gone' and makes use of both the Bb and F major related scales.

Herb Ellis

This passage was taken from 'Haystack Blues' by Herb Ellis, it uses the related scale of F Major.

Herb Ellis

Wes Montgomery

This fragment of improvisation comes from 'I don't Stand a Ghost of a Chance' and is built from the C major related scale.

Ike Isaacs with Wes Montgomery

Joe Pass

Joe Pass

This passage is from the melody of Joe's own tune 'Catch Me' and it uses the related scale of D minor.

Miles Davies

This solo comes from the tune 'Boplicity' from the historic Birth of the Cool recording session (1949) it is constructed from the F major related scale.

Charlie Parker

Both of these extracts stick rigidly to the use of related scales. Example one is a section of the riff from 'Red Cross' and it uses the G major scale. The second example comes from the blues tune 'Perhaps' and uses the A and D major related scales.

This particular phrase comes from the beginning of Charlie Parker's theme to 'Ornithology' and is built out of the related scales of E major and E minor.

Charlie Christian

Charlie Christian was one of the first players to popularize the related scale approach, for, with the development of amplification, he was able to play saxophone-style single note improvisations and still be heard above the rest of the band. The two examples here are illustrations of this style. The first is from 'I've found a new baby' and uses the D minor related chord with the exception of a B♮ passing note in the last bar.

The second example is from a blues recorded with Benny Goodman. This uses an F major related scale.

Jim Hall

Passages A and B are taken from Jim Hall's solo on the tune 'The Way You Look Tonight'. Both extracts use the same chord progression and the related scales are bars 1-2 F major, bar 3 G melodic minor, bar 4 C major, bar 5 F major. Bar 6 is very interesting in that the first example does the obvious by using a G major related scale over the D7 chord emphasizing the F♯ note whilst example B substitutes an F major chord for the usual D7 chord, the melodic line is then conceived in F major and the related scale of F is used. Besides being musically very satisfying this ingenious move prepared us for a smooth entry into the following G minor chord as both scales have a note in common, B♭.

You may have noticed by now that the same note is often duplicated in two or more related scales and if these happen to follow each other then it is usual to use the common note as a connection. There are countless examples of this in most people's jazz playing for it gives a good feeling of continuity — we do not want our improvisations to sound like a series of scales one after the other so the use of common notes should be explored as soon as you are familiar with the basic related scales. Here are some examples of common note connections by leading players to help you:

Django Reinhardt

Django Reinhardt

This extract from 'Minor Swing' uses the A minor and E major related scales. The common notes which link them together are the A at the end of the second bar and the B at the beginning of the third.

This extract is from the tune 'Undecided' and uses the related scales of C, E and A major (The common notes are bracketed).

Jim Hall

Another extract from Jim Hall's solo on 'The Way You Look Tonight' shows how well the use of common notes gives the feeling of continuity. Charlie Parker could play through the most complex chord changes with tremendous continuity and at it's highest level the art of improvising with related scales can create endless variation, excitement and above all surprise. Listen to any of the Charlie Parker records on the Dial or Savoy Labels, and if possible listen also to the trumpet player Clifford Brown who could play through any chord progression with amazing ease and good taste, regardless of tempo!

However the acknowledged masterpiece of scalic improvisation is John Coltrane's 'Giant Steps' (Atlantic 1311) several bars from this are included here for your own analysis.

John Coltrane

Charlie Byrd　　　*Barney Kessel*　　　*Herb Ellis*

THE PENTATONIC SCALE

The pentatonic is a five note scale constructed from major 2nds and minor 3rds. It contains no semitones and therefore no conventional leading note:

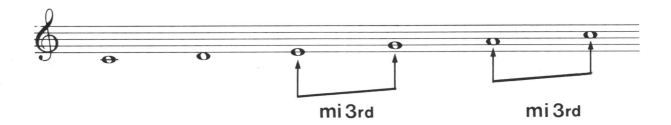

Like the augmented and diminished scale it can be inverted. There are five possible inversions:

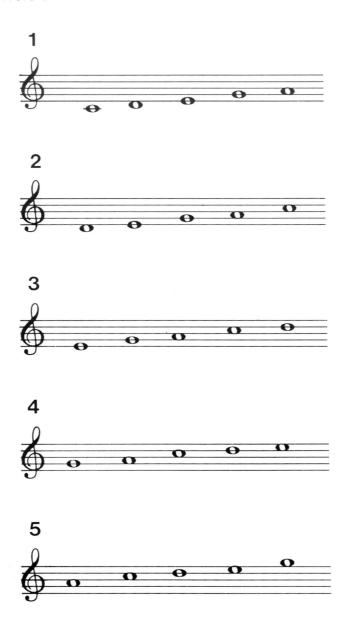

As with major and minor scales a pentatonic can be constructed on each note of the Key Cycle:

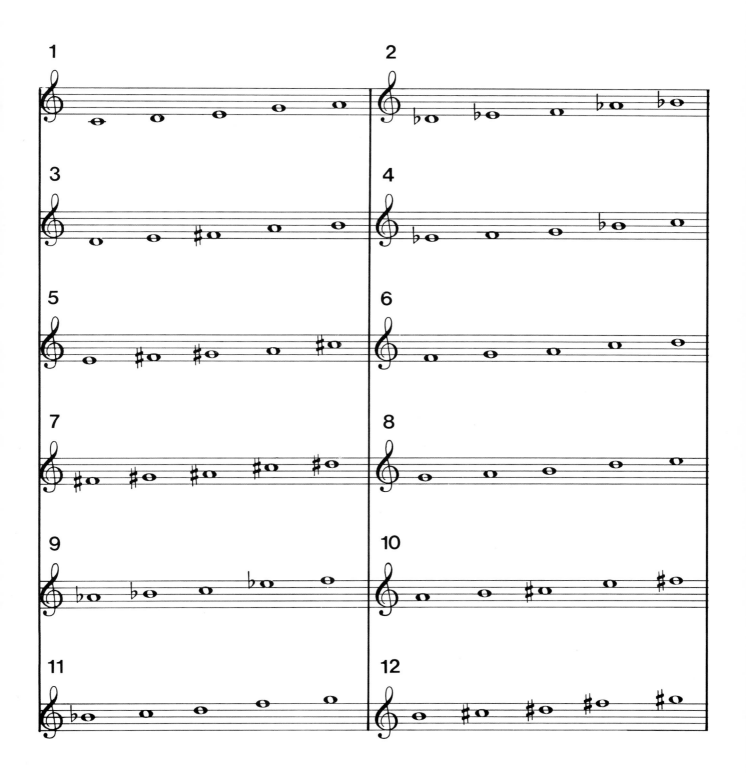

*You may find pentatonic scales easier to learn by thinking of them as major scales with the fourth and seventh notes omitted.

Many beautiful tunes have been made from the pentatonic scale, classical composers such as Dvorak and Debussy used it in some of their compositions and the younger generation of jazz musicians such as Herbie Hancock, Wayne Shorter, Keith Jarret, Chick Corea and guitarists Pat Martino and Larry Coryell have all used it in their improvisations.

Listen to Miles Smiles by Miles Davies on Columbia CS 9481 particularly Wayne Shorter's solo on Ginger Bread Boy which makes use of pentatonics, also Chick Corea's record Now He Sings, Now He Sobs, Solid State SS18039.

The beginning of Wayne Shorter's first chorus from 'Ginger Bread Boy':

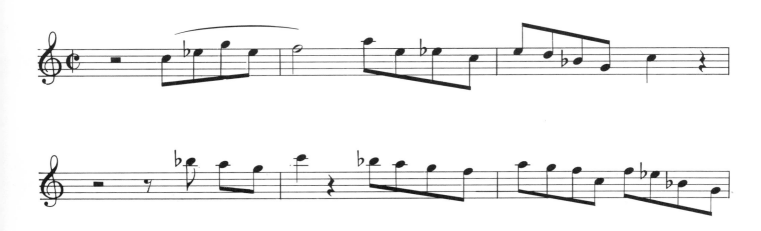

MODES

A mode is simply another word for a scale, though from the seven modes available only two have been fully exploited the Ionian (major scale) and the Aeolian (old minor scale). Until quite recently the remaining five have been ignored!

The feeling amongst many musicians that the major and minor scales are restricting has led to experiments with new tonal systems. Arnold Schoenberg developed an atonal system based upon the twelve notes of the chromatic scale which had no specific key centre, Stravinsky used bi-tonality, the juxtaposition of two different keys, while some composers such as Ravel, Manuel De Falla, and Vaughn Williams made use of the ancient modes to create a purer, less contrived music than their romantic predecessors.

The development of jazz has also seen a similar reaction to the traditional major/minor key system.

Two major figures in the breakdown of the old system were Ornette Coleman who abandoned keys altogether and Miles Davies who pioneered the current revival in the use of modes.

The tune 'So What' from Miles Davies' record 'Kind of Blue' had a tremendous impact amongst jazz players for although it is basically a simple 32 bar tune with question and answer phrases (between the bass and the group). It is constructed entirely from the Dorian mode. The effect of this is to eliminate the necessity of playing over a set pattern of chord changes, this gives the impression of space and a floating feeling. Hence from the limitations of a mode and it's inversions greater freedom for improvisational creativity (particularly rhythmic) exists: On this particular tune Miles Davies stays fairly close to the notes of the mode whilst John Coltrane wanders far away from it using chromatically altered notes and related scales.

THE SEVEN MODES

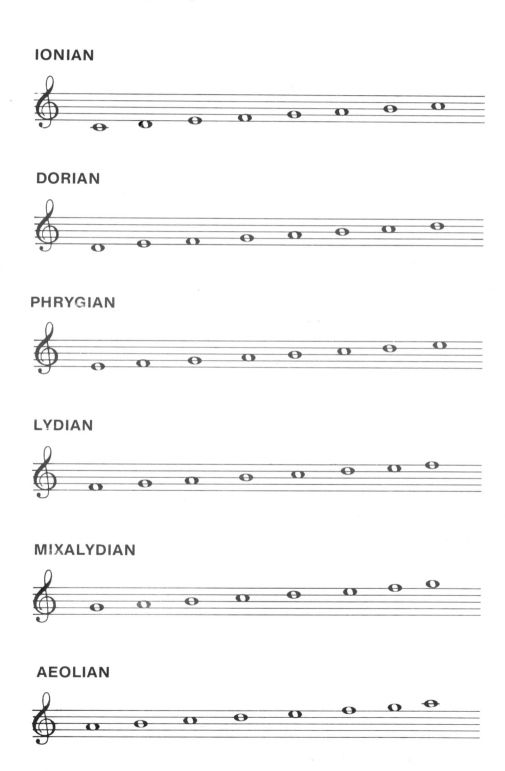

IONIAN

DORIAN

PHRYGIAN

LYDIAN

MIXALYDIAN

AEOLIAN

LOCRIAN

In the time of the ancient Greeks when modes formed the foundation of all civilised music chromatic instruments had not been developed and these seven modes could not be transposed into different keys, however today these scales may be played in every key.

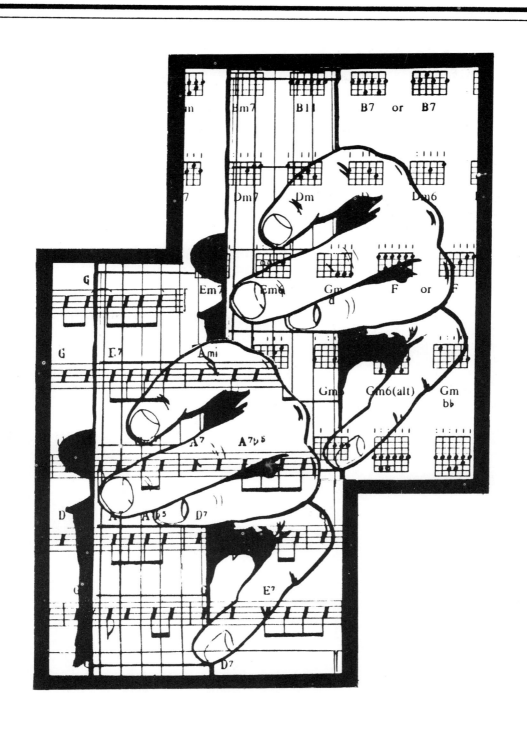

CHORD
PLAYING

THE PRACTICAL APPLICATION OF CHORDS

SECTION TWO

It is not essential to be able to read music for this section of the book, though it is useful to know the names of the various notes on the fingerboard.

If you do not know the names of the notes on the fingerboard, the following chart should help you. It is intended for reference only and need not be memorized.

Barney Kessel

FINGERBOARD CHART

BASIC BARRE CHORDS

Before you learn some of those beautiful close harmony jazz chords, it is essential to come to terms with the basic bar chords.

Although these chords are not used a good deal in jazz, they are used extensively in most other popular music and they form a very useful point of departure for the jazz guitarist.

CHORDS BUILT FROM THE 'F' SHAPE

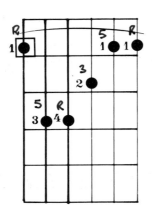

MAJOR

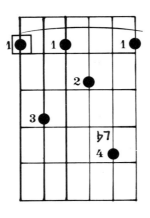

7th

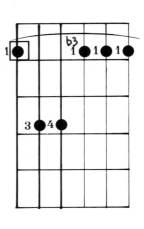

MINOR

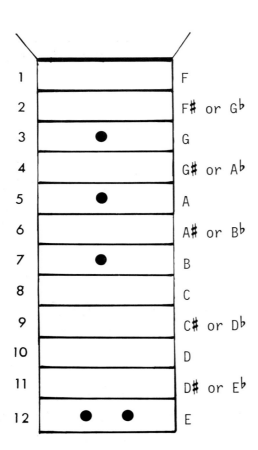

This chart shows which chord is formed when the root is played on a specific fret, i.e., when the 1st finger is barring the 5th fret the resulting chord will be A (if you know the names of the notes on the 6th string, the chords take their name from the note. If not, refer to the fingerboard chart).

■ = Root Note

*This chart works the same for the 7th and the minor shapes above.

Practice the following sequences, using the Barre Chords given.

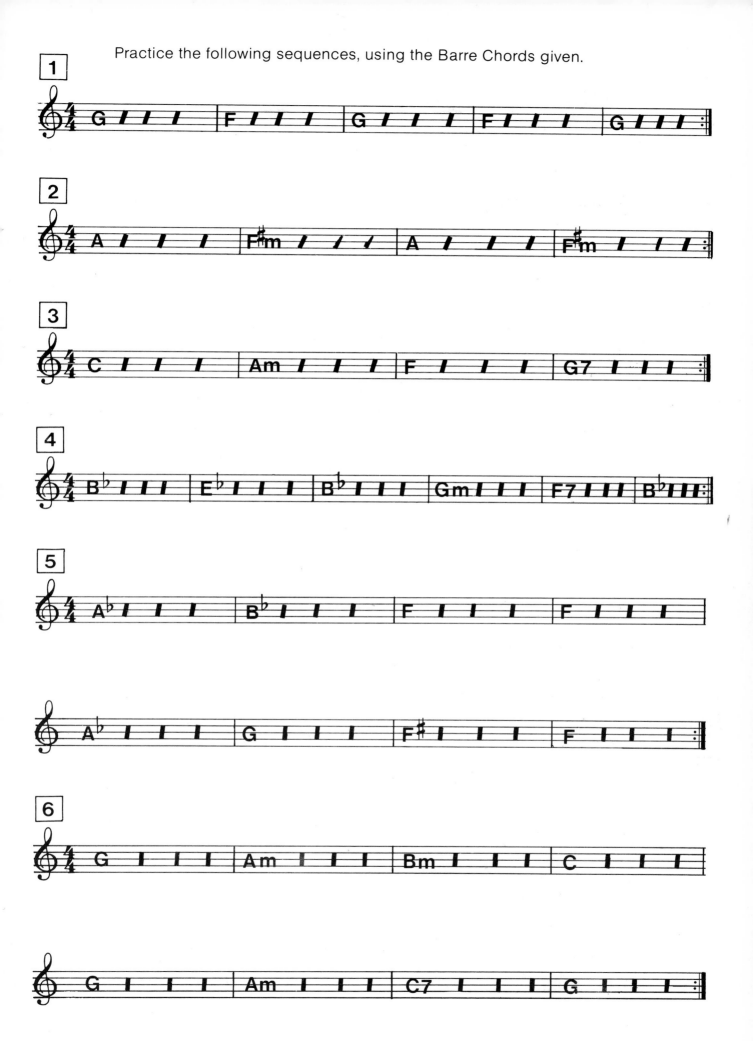

Now try playing some of the tunes that you already know using these three chord shapes.

CHORDS BUILT FROM THE B♭ SHAPE

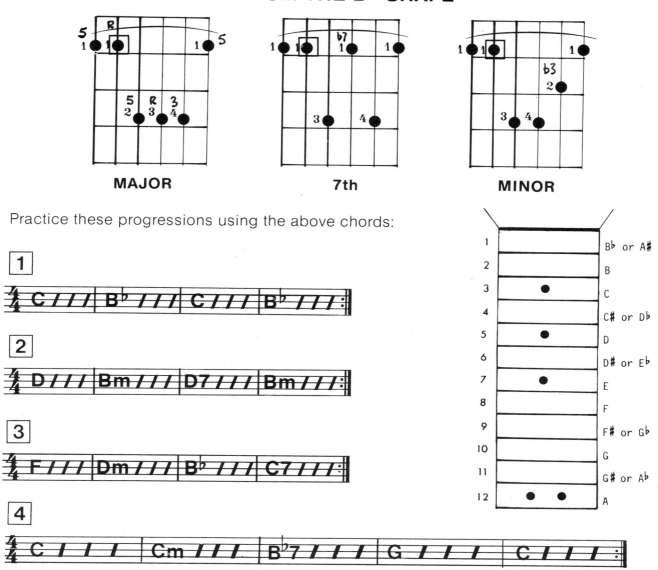

MAJOR   **7th**   **MINOR**

Practice these progressions using the above chords:

1
| 𝄴 C / / / | B♭ / / / | C / / / | B♭ / / / :|

2
| 𝄴 D / / / | Bm / / / | D7 / / / | Bm / / / :|

3
| 𝄴 F / / / | Dm / / / | B♭ / / / | C7 / / / :|

4
| 𝄴 C / / / | Cm / / / | B♭7 / / / | G / / / | C / / / :|

PRACTICE PROGRESSIONS

Using the six bar chords that you have learnt, work out how many different ways you can find to play the following progressions.

1
| 𝄴 C / / / | Am / / / | G / / / | G7 / / / :|

2
| 𝄴 C / / / | A / / / | F / / / | Fm / / / | G7 / / / :|

3
| 𝄴 G / / / | Em / / / | C / / / | Cm / / / | D7 / / / :|

Try moving these progressions into different keys. Listen hard to the different quality of sound produced by inversions of a chord with the same name. By making a mental note of the sound produced by a particular shape of a chord, you are training your ears to observe small but important differences in sound, these differences, created by re-arranging the notes of a chord in a slightly different order (inverting them) are known as chord *voicings.*

As you progress you will find that the voicing of chords is of great importance. Even a string of basic triads can sound effective if the voices (notes) flow smoothly from one chord to the next.

MORE BASIC MOVEABLE CHORD SHAPES

Most of the chords that you will be learning are in fact moveable and providing that you can remember which note is the root of the chord from which it takes it's name, then you should find little difficulty in working out which particular chord is formed on a specific fret.

Below are some more basic major, minor and 7th chords that I would like you to learn before going any further:

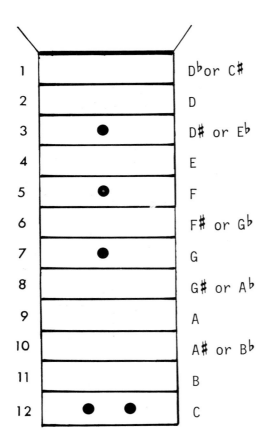

Major shape with root note on 2nd and 5th strings

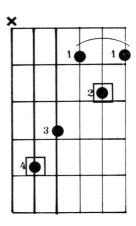

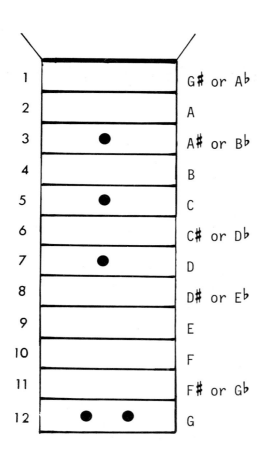

1	G♯ or A♭
2	A
3 ●	A♯ or B♭
4	B
5 ●	C
6	C♯ or D♭
7 ●	D
8	D♯ or E♭
9	E
10	F
11	F♯ or G♭
12 ● ●	G

Major shape with root note on the 1st and 3rd strings

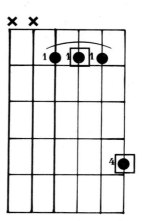

These charts show what the chord is called when the first finger is covering the numbered fret, not necessarily the root is on that fret.

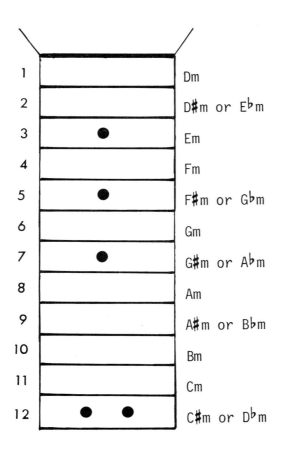

1	Dm
2	D♯m or E♭m
3 ●	Em
4	Fm
5 ●	F♯m or G♭m
6	Gm
7 ●	G♯m or A♭m
8	Am
9	A♯m or B♭m
10	Bm
11	Cm
12 ● ●	C♯m or D♭m

Minor shape with root note on 2nd string

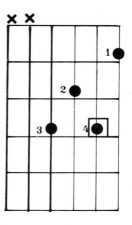

7th CHORDS

When you move these new 7th chords up and down the fingerboard be careful not to sound the strings marked with an X.

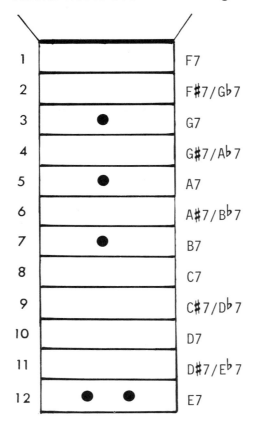

Fret	Chord
1	F7
2	F#7/Gb7
3	G7
4	G#7/Ab7
5	A7
6	A#7/Bb7
7	B7
8	C7
9	C#7/Db7
10	D7
11	D#7/Eb7
12	E7

7th shape with root note on 6th string

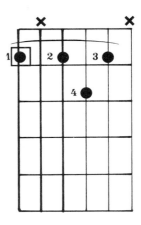

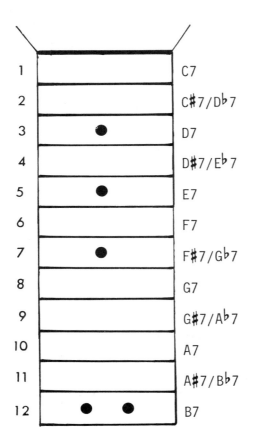

Fret	Chord
1	C7
2	C#7/Db7
3	D7
4	D#7/Eb7
5	E7
6	F7
7	F#7/Gb7
8	G7
9	G#7/Ab7
10	A7
11	A#7/Bb7
12	B7

7th shape with root note on 2nd and 5th strings

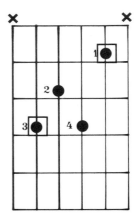

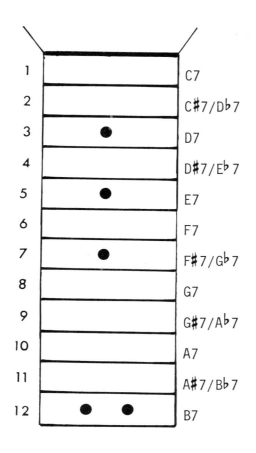

1	C7
2	C#7/Db7
3	D7
4	D#7/Eb7
5	E7
6	F7
7	F#7/Gb7
8	G7
9	G#7/Ab7
10	A7
11	A#7/Bb7
12	B7

7th shape with root note on 2nd string

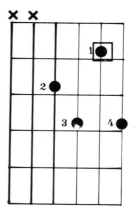

The third chord here is a variant of the second one, compare them both by listening carefully to the voicing of each. The chord with the root on the fifth string is full and bassy but lacks bite, while the chord with the extra note on the first string is capable of cutting through a large jazz orchestra or a thick organ sound.

As success with chords depends on how you use them, you must continuously listen to the quality of sound produced by the shapes, by doing this you will be well on the way to using the right chord at the right time.

Remember, the ability to play good jazz depends as much on your ears as it does on your fingers.

Here are two blues progressions which use these new 7th chords:

Listen carefully to the voicing of each chord. Notice how, even with careful use of the 7th chord only, we can maintain a certain amount of interest and creativity.

BLUES IN G

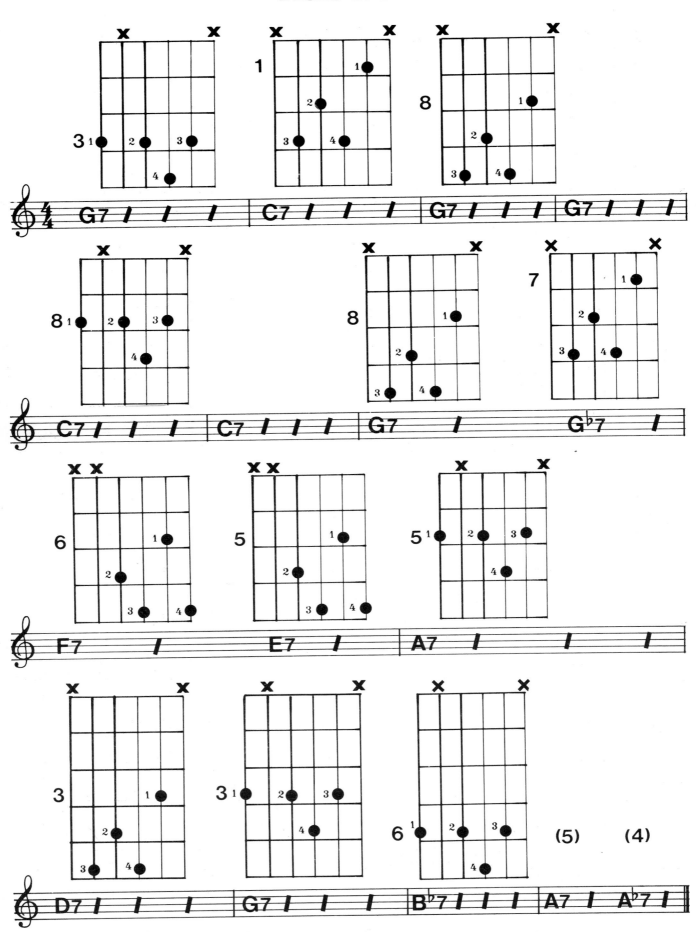

BLUES IN B♭

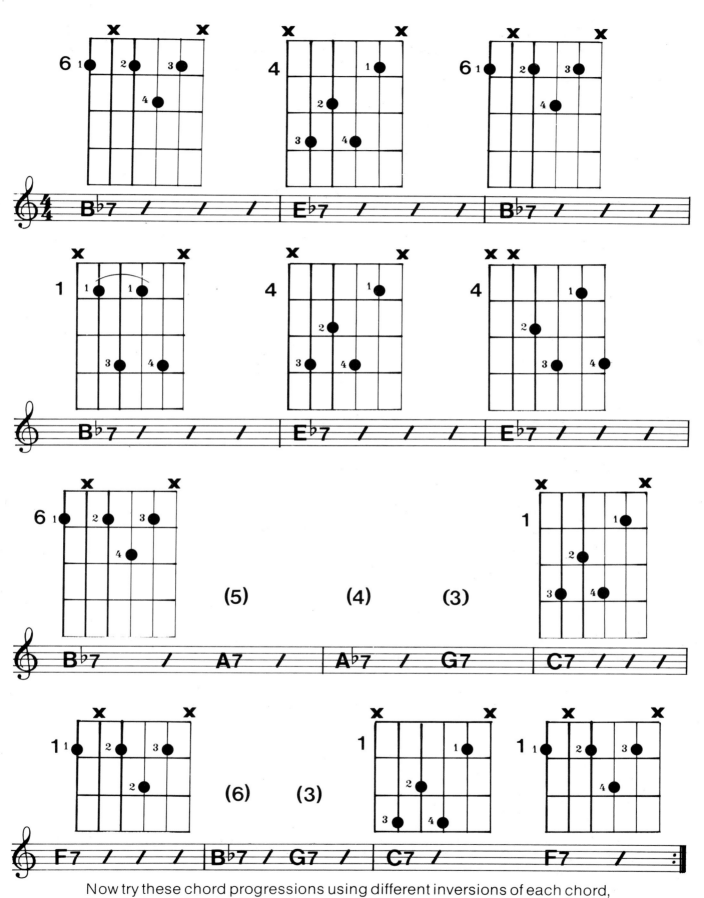

Now try these chord progressions using different inversions of each chord, listening carefully to the particular voicings of each.

When you have done this, work out your progressions in different keys.

MORE PROGRESSIONS USING MOVEABLE 7th CHORDS

Progressions of 7ths like this one are frequently used in modern jazz, they can be described by any of the following names.

cycle of 4ths
cycle of 5ths
back-cycling
the cycle of keys
circle of 5ths

Each of these definitions is actually quite correct. What each definition really means is that the root of each chord is either a 5th higher or a 4th lower than the previous chord root.

Whatever point we begin our progression at doesn't really matter, for if you follow the pattern through you will eventually pass through every key, hence the definition cycle or circle.

The following diagram should make this clear.

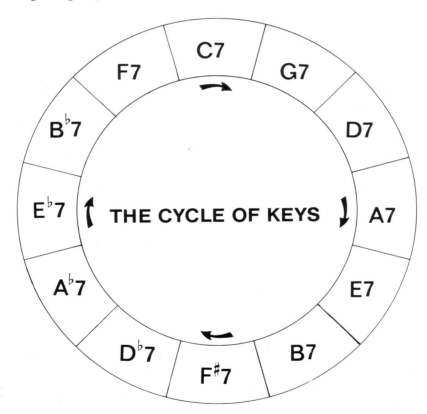

Many of the 'standard' tunes favoured by the jazz guitarists employ sections from the cycle as do many jazz originals like Thelonius Monk's 'Round Midnight'. Good examples can be found in All The Things You Are, Autumn Leaves, Cherokee, and John Coltrane's Giant Steps.

TWO 7th CHORDS VOICED ON THE TREBLE STRINGS

By voicing your 7th chords in this way it is possible to use them in your own chord solos. They also penetrate and punctuate well when you are involved in chord accompaniment.

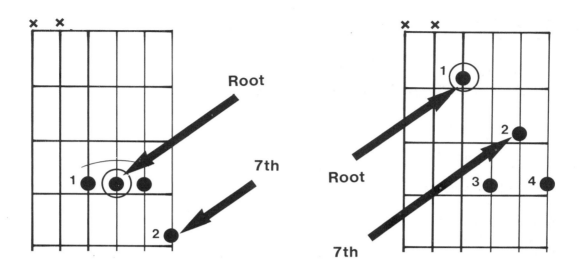

Both of these chords can be easily altered, making them ideal for chord melody playing.

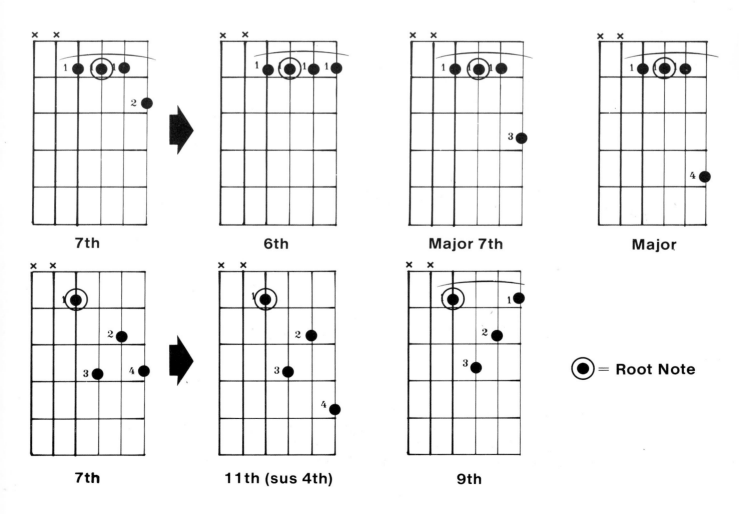

Try substituting some of these altered chords in place of the basic 7th chord, especially where a 7th chord is repeated for two or more bars. Listen carefully to the effect of this substitution and memorize all of the successful combinations so that you can use them when the need arises.

BLUES PROGRESSION USING ALTERED CHORDS

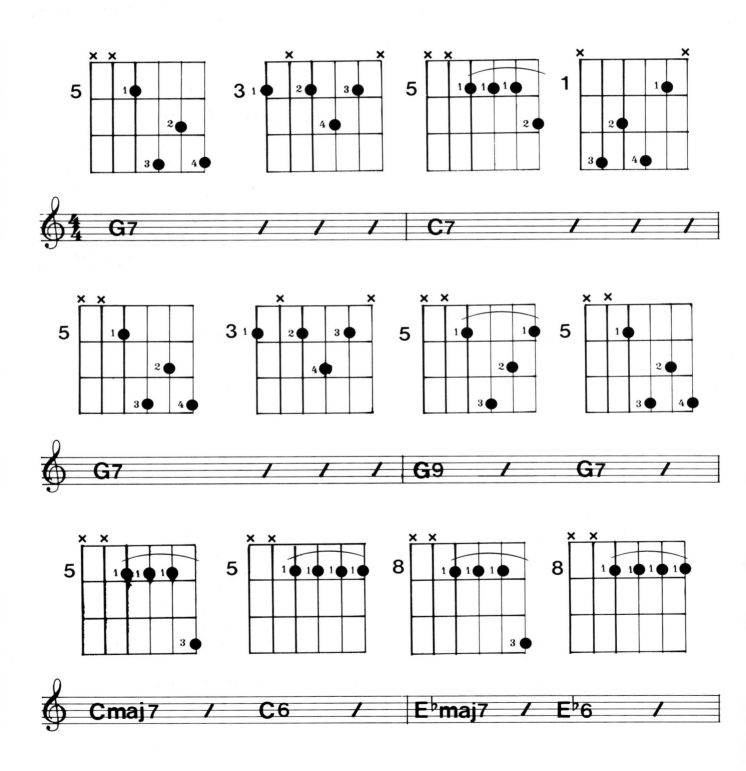

cont.

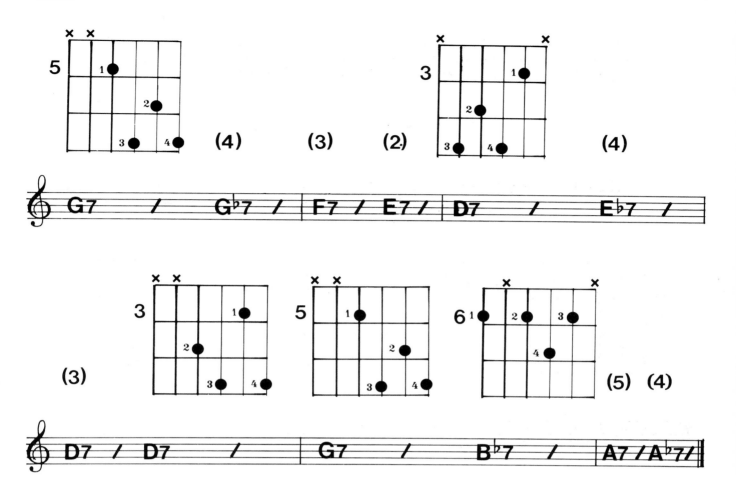

When you can play this fluently, listen to the way each individual note within a chord progresses to the next note on the same string in the following chord. Jazz musicians call this 'voice leading' and many interesting melodies can be found hidden away in even the simplest of chord progressions.

CHORDS USING A 3rd FINGER BARRE

Some jazz chords employ the difficult technique of flattening the third finger to cover three or more strings. This is a difficult technique to acquire and it requires much perseverance and continuous hard practice!

You may find it re-assuring to know that many professional classical guitar players who have spent years acquiring a sound technique find this particular technique incredibly difficult. The reason for this being that it is seldom used in the classical guitar repertoire, and that the third finger barre technique is so alien to other facets of technique that it demands special treatment, determined effort and hard work even for a highly skilled performer to perfect!

The most popular chord to employ this technique is the ninth. With the aid of the fingerboard chart you should be able to work out the names of this shape up and down the neck.

9th CHORD

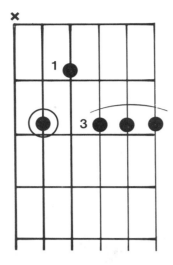

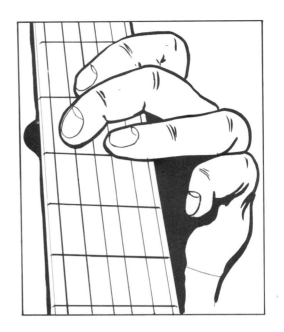

This particular chord is usually substituted for the basic 7th chord or combined together with it to give a greater variety of voicings. It can be used in either major or minor keys with good effect.

Practice the following progression from the cycle of 5ths and experiment with your voicing of 7th chords now that you have a few alternatives to choose from.

Practice progression using the new ninth chord and a sequence from the cycle of 5ths.

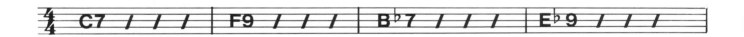

$\frac{4}{4}$ | C7 / / / | F9 / / / | B♭7 / / / | E♭9 / / /

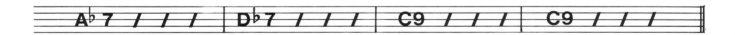

A♭7 / / / | D♭7 / / / | C9 / / / | C9 / / /

Blues progression using 9ths only: **ADE'S BOOGIE**

$\frac{4}{4}$ | G9 / / / | C9 / / / | G9 / / / | G9 / / /

C9 / / / | C9 / / / | C9 / G9 / | F9 / E9 /

D9 / / / | C9 / / / | G9 / B♭9 / | A9 / A♭9 /

THE NINTH CHORD WITH EXTENSIONS

This particular ninth chord shape lends itself well to extensions because the 4th finger is not required for the basic shape, leaving it free to add new notes as required.

The obvious and most frequently used extension is that of the added 13th, making the most popular 13th chord shape used in jazz.

13th CHORD

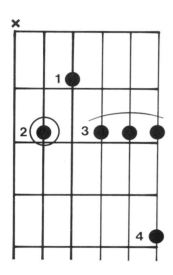

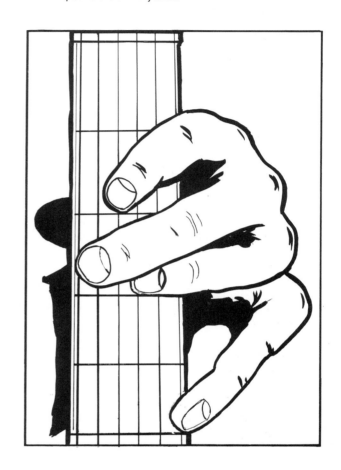

This 13th chord may be substituted for a 9th or 7th chord in the major key and is particularly effective as a substitute for the dominant chord in a minor key.

ADE'S BOOGIE (coloured with 13ths)

$\frac{4}{4}$ | G13 / G9 / | C13 / C9 / | G13 / G9 / | G13 / G9 / |

| C13 / C9 / | C13 / C9 / | C13 / G♭9 / | F13 / E9 / |

| D9 / D13 / | C13 / C9 / | G9 / B♭9 / | A9 / A♭9 / |

The extended 13th note can also be used as a passing note to decorate the 9th chord, particularly when the 9th chord is held for more than one bar of music.

The most popular method of decorating the 9th chord is to move the 4th finger in semitones (distances of one fret) between the 13th chord and the 9th chord as illustrated.

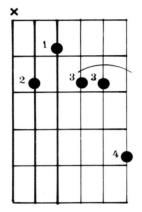 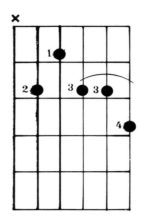 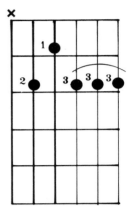

Practice these chords in the above order, at first using four beats for each chord, gradually increasing the speed until you can execute the changes using a chord on every beat.

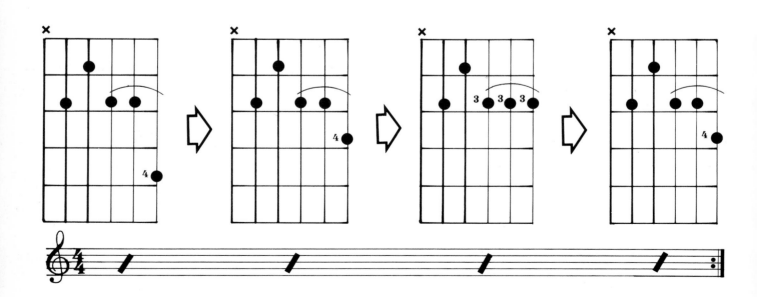

Other popular ninth chord extensions are:

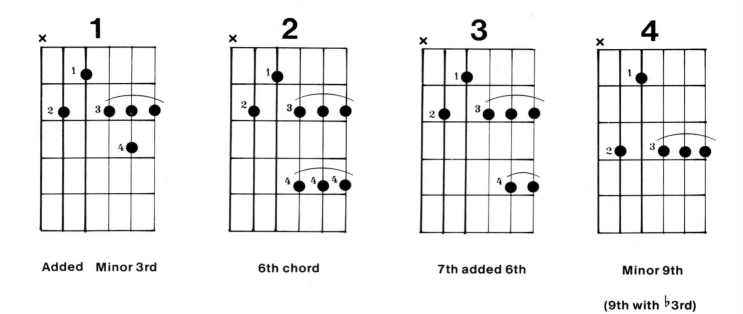

| Added Minor 3rd | 6th chord | 7th added 6th | Minor 9th |

(9th with ♭3rd)

CHORD 1

The 9th with the added minor 3rd (1) is used a good deal in jazz-rock styles and it works equally well in major or minor keys, it has also been used in atonal (no specific key) and polytonal (many different keys) music. A great favourite with such diverse stylists as Jimi Hendrix, John McLaughlin and Pat Martino.

CHORDS 2 AND 3

These chords are basically used in passing, to decorate the basic 9th and 13th chord. Many of the Chicago blues guitarists use chord 2 to alternate with a basic chord, resulting in a rocking boogie style similar to Chuck Berry.

CHORD 4

The minor 9th chord is one of the most beautiful and effective chords that is played on the guitar. It can be substituted for a basic minor or minor 7th chord, but it requires careful use in the major keys. Many of the chord solos by the jazz guitarist Johnny Smith employ this chord.

MORE 9th CHORD SHAPES

As the 9th chord is considered an essential chord for the jazz player, it is useful to know as many different shapes and their voicings as possible. Here are some of the most popular ones:

MORE 9th CHORD SHAPES

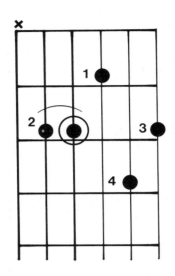 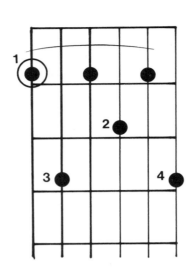 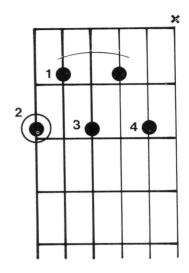

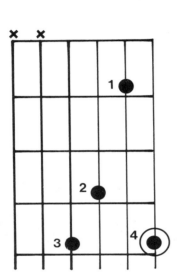 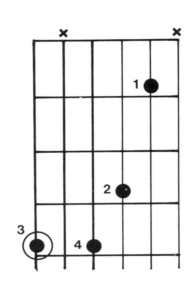 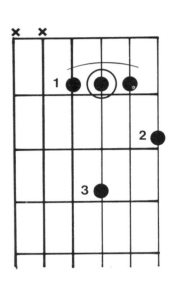

PRACTICE PROGRESSIONS

1

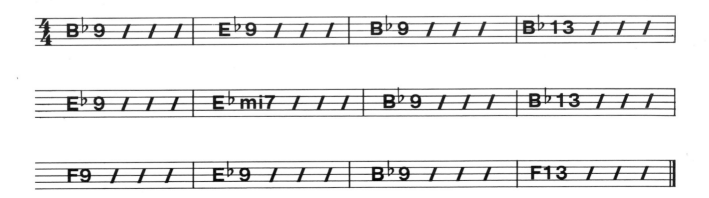

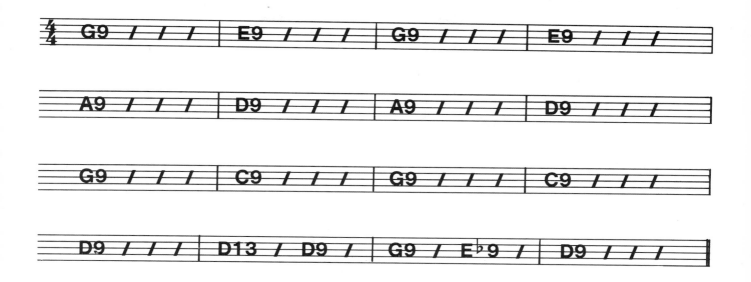

SEE SEE RIDER

THE MINOR 7th AND MINOR 6th

These chords again use the third finger barre technique and as they are often used together it is a good idea to practice changing from one to the other.

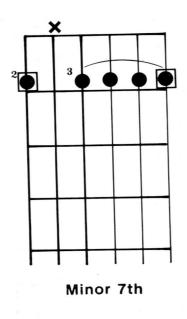

Minor 7th

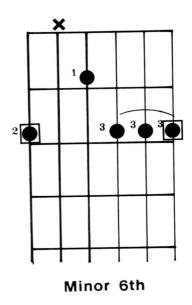

Minor 6th

PRACTICE PROGRESSIONS

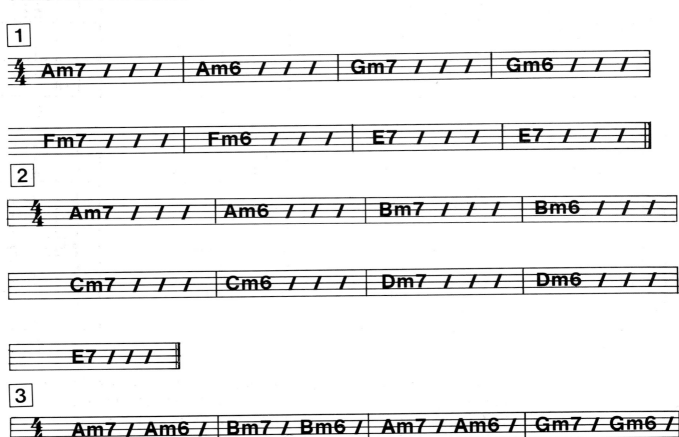

Transpose into different keys.

MINOR 6th AND 7th EXTENSIONS

The same extensions as those used on the 9th chord are available.

MORE MINOR 6th AND 7th SHAPES

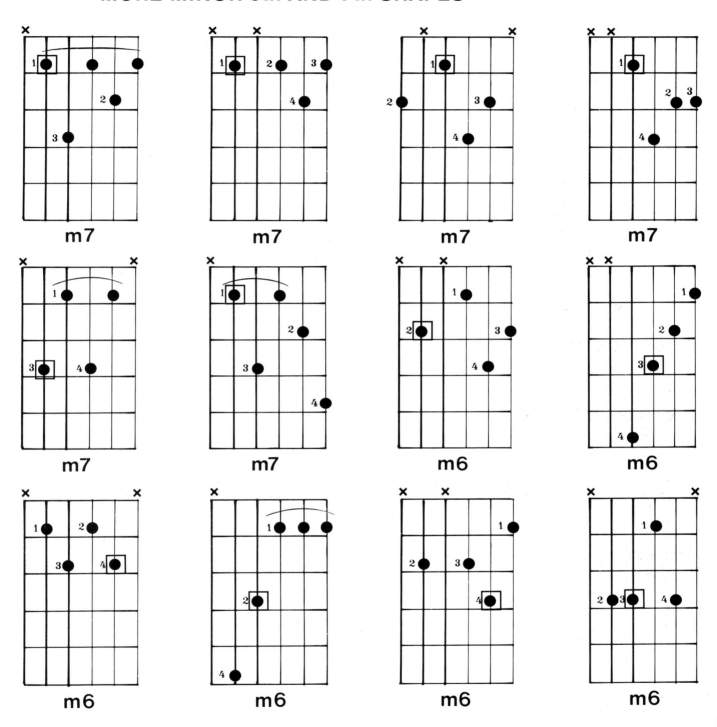

The best way to master these new shapes is to pair a m6th and a m7th shape together, limiting yourself to these two shapes only. Do this with each minor 6th and 7th shape in turn, when you can make these changes quite smoothly, try different combinations until facility is gained with all of the shapes. As with all of your previous chord shapes listen carefully to the particular voicing of each one so that your ear will eventually suggest which shape to use at a specific point in a tune. Hearing a sound in your head and instantly reproducing it on the guitar is what jazz is all about.

ST. JAMES INFIRMARY

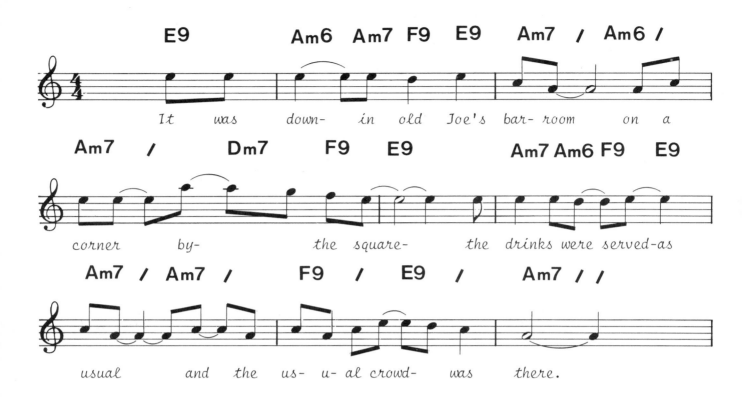

E9		Am6 Am7 F9 E9	Am7 / Am6 /

It was down- in old Joe's bar- room on a

Am7 /	Dm7 F9 E9	Am7 Am6 F9 E9

corner by- the square- the drinks were served-as

Am7 / Am7 /	F9 / E9 /	Am7 / /

usual and the us- u- al crowd- was there.

THE 13th CHORD

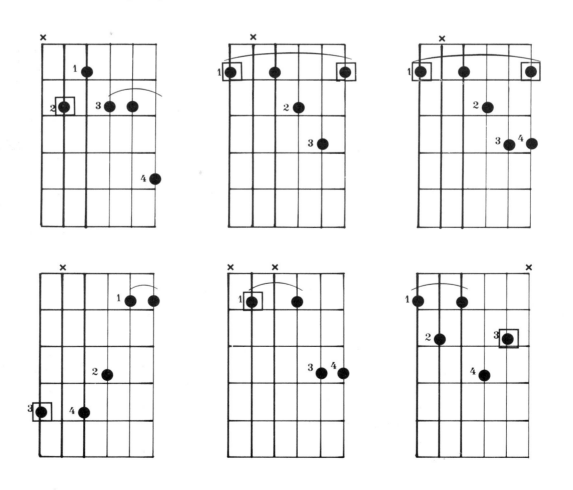

MAJOR 7th AND MAJOR 6th CHORDS

Like the 9th chord, the major 7th is widely used by jazz guitarists, it is often combined with the major 6th chord to be used as substitutes for a basic major chord.

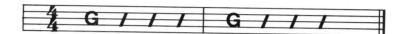

in a jazz idiom would be:

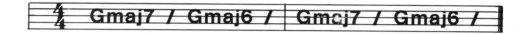

Major 7th chords (maj 7)

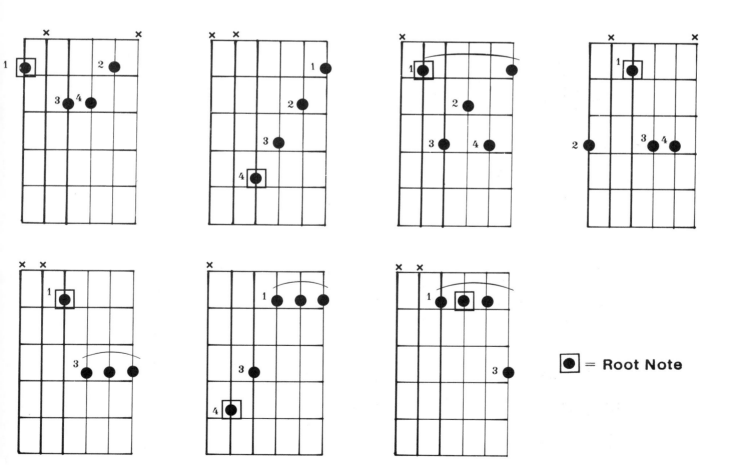

Major 6th chords (Maj 6)

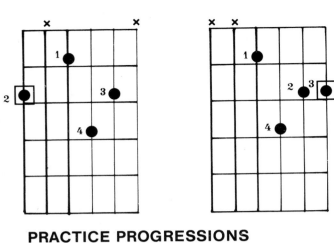
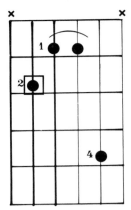
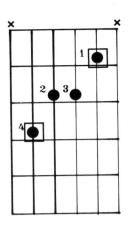

PRACTICE PROGRESSIONS

1

| $\frac{4}{4}$ **Gmaj7** / / / | **Gmaj6** / / / | **Amaj7** / / / |

| **Amaj6** / / / | **Bim7** / / / | **Bmi6** / / / |

| **Ami7** / / / | **Ami6** / / / | **Gmaj7** / / / | **Gmaj6** / / / |

2

| $\frac{4}{4}$ **D13** / / / | **E13** / / / | **Amaj7** / / / |

| **Amaj6** / / / | **Ami7** / / / | **Ami6** / / / |

| **Gmaj7** / / / | **Gmaj6** / / / |

3

| $\frac{3}{4}$ **B♭maj7** / / | **B♭maj6** / / | **F13** / / | **F9** / / |

| **B♭mi7** / / | **B♭mi6** / / | **A♭maj7** / / | **A♭maj6** / / |

Transpose these progressions into (a) C major, (b) D major, (c) A major.

MINOR CHORD EXTENSIONS

When a minor, m6 or m7th chord is sustained for a few bars, interest may be created by the addition of extra notes.

By extending basic chords in this way we extend the possibilities for interesting chord voicings and we can also make use of any moving bass patterns that may arise.

Play the following minor chord extensions and listen carefully to the descending notes on the fourth string.

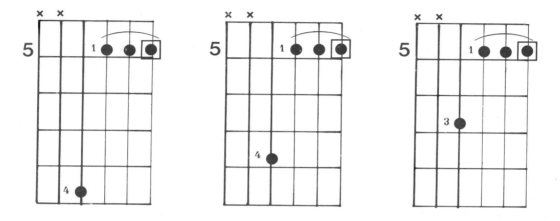

Moving bass patterns such as this one are very common as they relieve any feeling of monotony that may arise from a repeated chord. Progressions such as this can also lead tastefully on to another chord. For example in the following progression, minor chord extensions falling chromatically on the fourth string connect a basic minor chord (Am) to a 9th chord (D9).

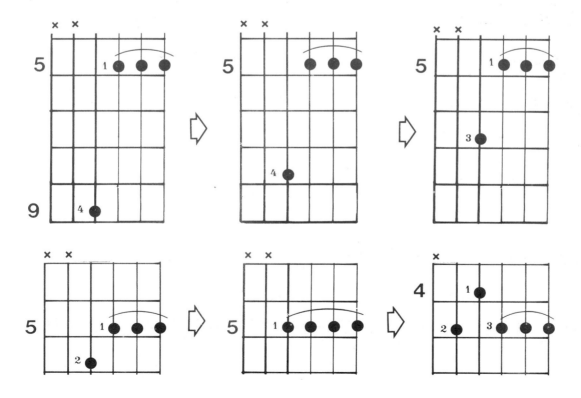

The descending chromatic notes formed on the fourth string could also lead to an Am6 chord:

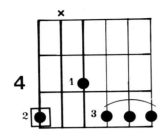

thus retaining the minor tonality.

MINOR CHORD EXTENSIONS

BASIC SHAPE:

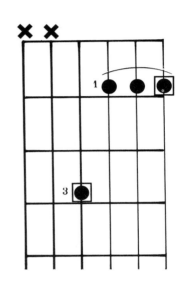

POSSIBLE EXTENSIONS:

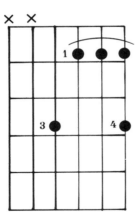
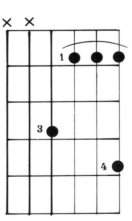
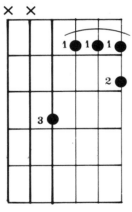
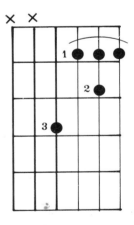

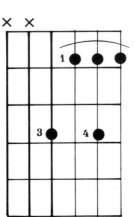
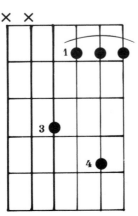
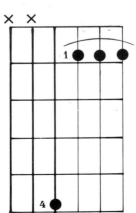
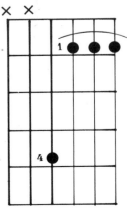

Minor chord extensions cont.

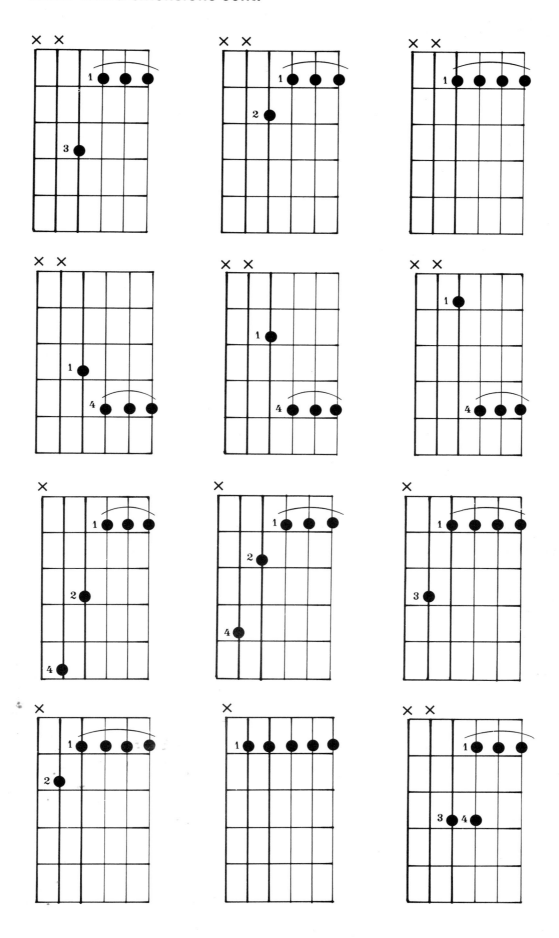

MINOR CHORD EXTENSIONS

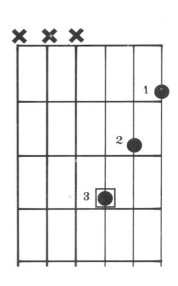

BASIC SHAPE

POSSIBLE EXTENSIONS

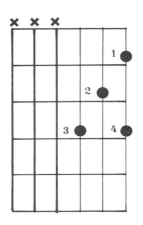
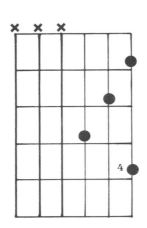
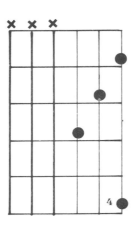
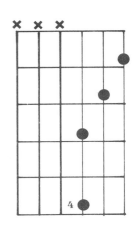

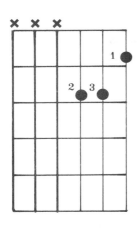
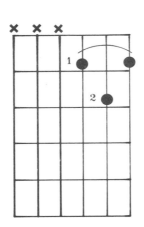
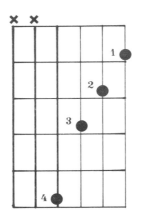
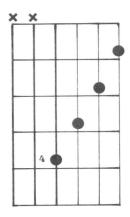

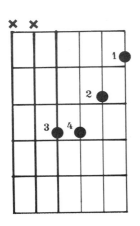
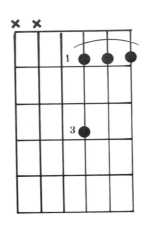

Many other chord shapes may also be extended in this way. Basic chord shapes generally afford more possibilities. The two major shapes are ideal for this purpose.

MAJOR CHORD EXTENSIONS

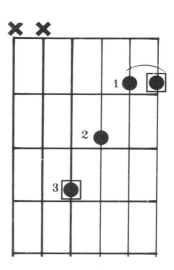

BASIC SHAPE

POSSIBLE EXTENSIONS

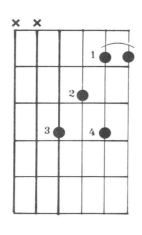
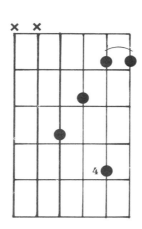
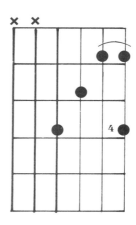

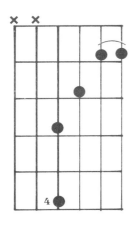
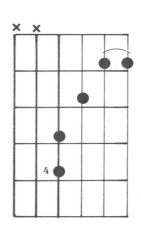
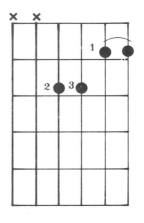

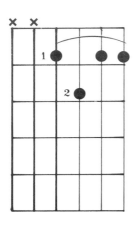
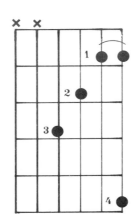
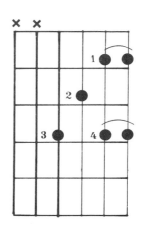

Major chord extensions cont.

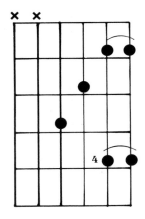 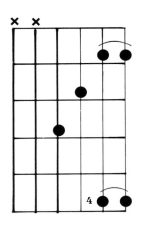 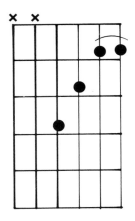

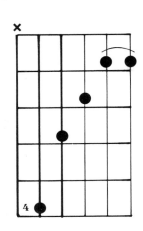 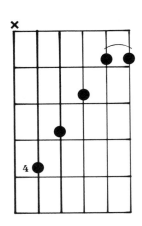 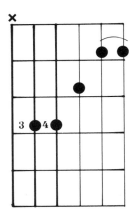

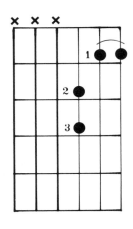 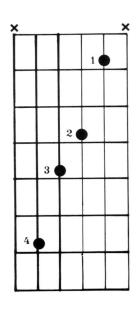 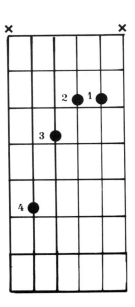

70

MAJOR CHORD EXTENSIONS

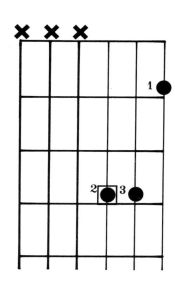

BASIC SHAPE:

POSSIBLE EXTENSIONS:

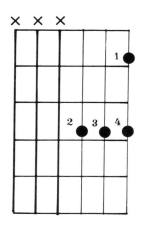
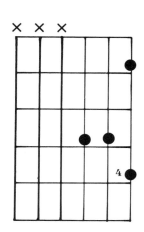
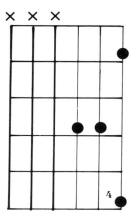
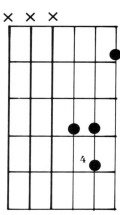

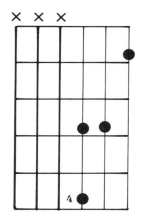
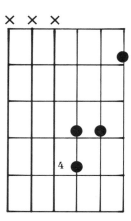
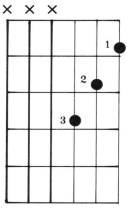
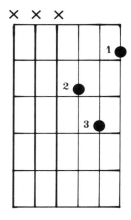

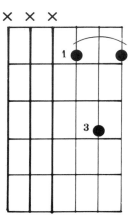
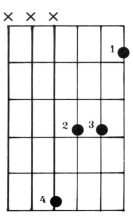
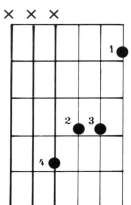
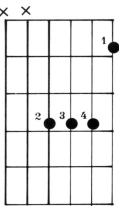

MAJOR CHORD EXTENSIONS CONT.

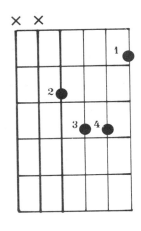
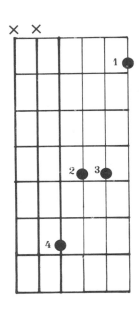
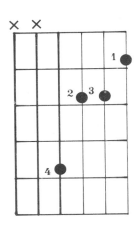

Try some of these chord extensions yourself, especially when you come up against a repeated chord.

The most common extensions are those which create a moving bass part like those in the sequence below:

MAJOR KEY

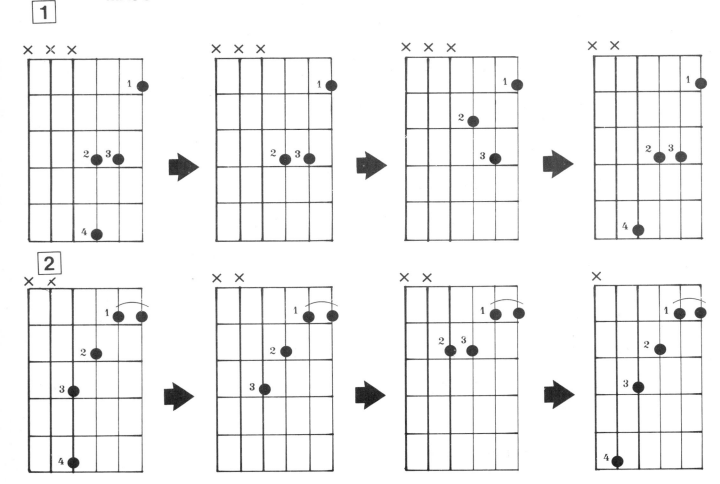

① MINOR KEY

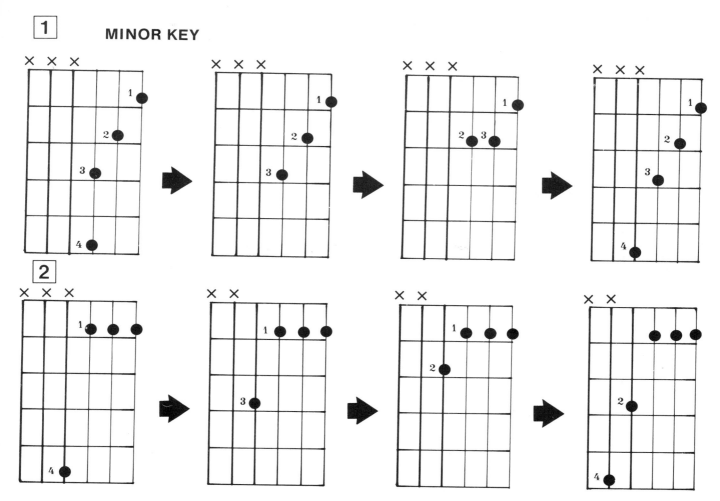

CHORD SUBSTITUTION

Chord substitution is generally employed when the same chord lasts for two or more bars. Using substitute chords adds colour and relieves any monotony that may otherwise occur. The basic reasons for the need for chord substitutions are explained in the first section of this book and can be summarized as follows:

1. **To create tension.**

2. **To create an element of surprise.**

3. **To extend the possibilities for improvisation.**

4. **To strengthen and add colour to a weak or uninteresting progression.**

Many devices may be used other than the changing of one chord for another.

Favourite techniques empoyed by jazz guitarists include:

1. **Stepwise (or semitone) movement.**

2. **Minor thirds.**

3. **Moving bass and cyclic chord sequences.**

4. **Pedal Point.**

Although these techniques are explained later on in this book, the basic art of substituting one chord for another must be your first step in coming to terms with jazz guitar chord playing.

The following table is useful for learning which chords may be used as substitutions:

7th Chord use any from 9th, 11th, 13th, ♯5th, ♭5th, ♭9th, ♯9th.

Major Chords use any from maj6th, maj7th, 9th relative mi7th.

Minor Chords use any from mi6th, mi7th, mi9th.

An example of this may be:

BASIC PROGRESSION

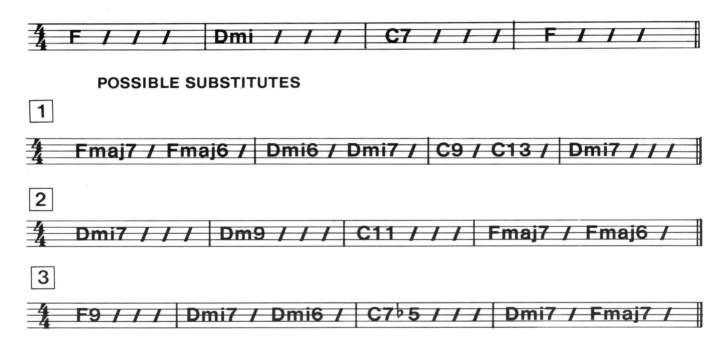

POSSIBLE SUBSTITUTES

Experiment with your own substitutions for this sequence, listed below are some new chord shapes which you will find are useful substitutes for a 7th chord.

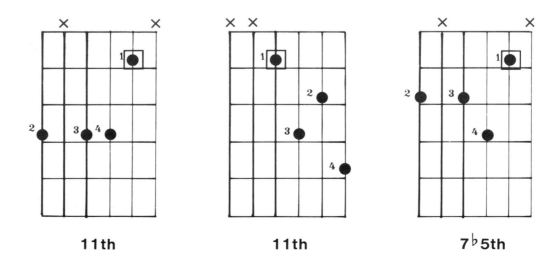

| 11th | 11th | 7♭5th |

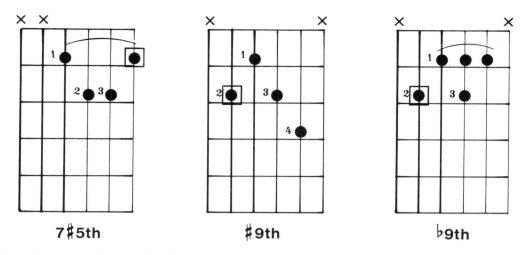

7♯5th   **♯9th**   **♭9th**

CHORD CONNECTION

When you know your basic substitute chords you can make the change from one substitute chord to another more interesting by the addition of new chords.

SEMITONE MOVEMENT

Any new chord may be approached from a semitone (one fret) above or below, e.g. if our basic change was:

We could approach the F9 chord in two different ways, from one fret above:

or one fret below:

Try connecting the following progressions by semitone movement using a new chord in place of the chord marked*.

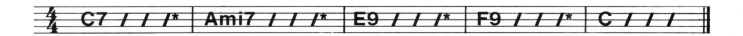

Now try semitone movement to connect chords in the tunes that you already know.

Other devices that may be used to connect chords together are:

1. The augmented chord, which connects dominant (V) to tonic (I) i.e.

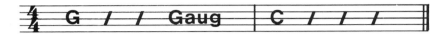

2. The diminished chord which connects sub-dominant (IV) to tonic (I),

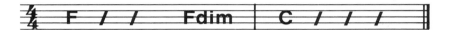

3. The minor chord which also connects the sub-dominant (IV) to the tonic (I).

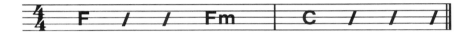

Note that all of these connections are in the key of C and the connecting chord has the same name as the chord used prior to the connection. Here are some examples in the key of F major.

This dominant to tonic chord change could be connected with an augmented chord:

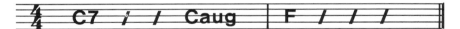

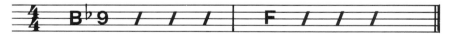

This sub-dominant to tonic chord change could be connected either by a minor chord

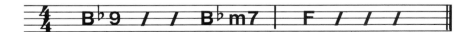

or by a diminished chord:

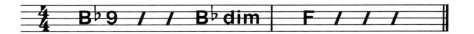

Memorize the following table:

V (dominant) to I (tonic) use Augmented chord.

IV (subdominant to I (tonic) use diminished or minor chord.

All other chords semitone movement.

There are other ways to connect chords together including the use of voice-leading which is a more advanced study. Several books are listed at the end of this chapter if you wish to pursue the subject in greater depth. The connections listed above are the ones in common use and are employed frequently by the great jazz guitarists.

MINOR THIRDS

The use of chord movement in minor 3rds is sometimes referred to as symmetric cycles and all this means is that a chord is moved up or down the fingerboard by distances of four frets (inclusive). By using one chord shape and moving it in this way we can give the impression of knowing an incredible number of chords!

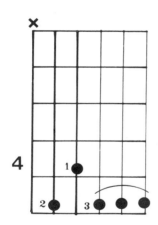

If you move the D9th shape up the fingerboard in minor 3rds the resulting sequence would be:

D9, F9, A♭9, B9.

This device may be used when a chord is sustained for at least a bars duration and the above sequence would add tension and colour to a bar of D7 or D9.

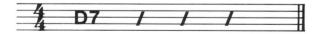

Could be:

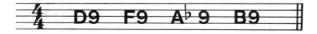

or in reverse, descending in minor 3rds from the thirteenth fret.

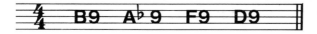

Most jazz guitarists use this device to some extent, particularly Joe Pass and Tal Farlow. The chords favoured by Tal Farlow are the 9th and Mi7th.

9th　　　　　　　　　　　**MINOR 7th**

Here is a tyical Farlow chord change in descending minor 3rds:

(11th fret)　　　　　　(8th fret)　　　　　　(5th fret)

This sequence would be played over a bar of D7 or D9. There are many good examples of progressions in minor 3rds on the LP 'The Red Norvo Trio' Savoy 2212 (the trio being Red Norvo, Tal Farlow and Charlie Mingus).

PEDALS

A pedal note is one that is repeated several times, usually in the bass part, while the chord sequence continues to move. Pedals are used effectively by jazz guitarists not only as substitutions but also for introductions, bridge passages and endings. Many of the *standard tunes* favoured by jazz guitarists also make use of it, for example 'Green Dolphin Street' and 'My Foolish Heart' both use a pedal note as the bass part whilst 'Here's That Rainy Day' and 'One Note Samba' use a pedal note as the melody.

There are endless variations of this device and it is my aim to show you some of the more common ones, beginning with chord changes built around a sustained melody note in the top part of a chord. I will give these all in the key of C for ease of writing, but remember to try them out in many different keys so that they eventually become second nature.

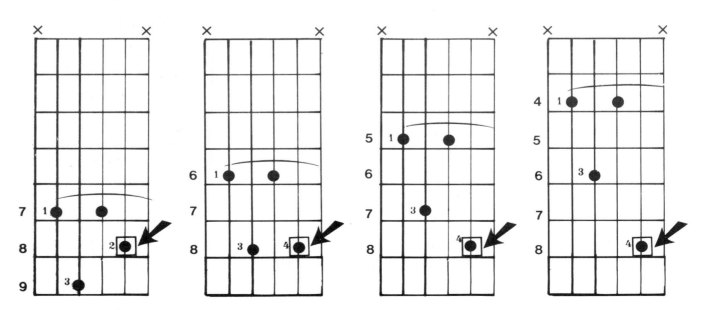

The late Charles Mingus, jazz bassist and composer who had a particular fondness for the use of pedals.

The pedal note here is the G on the second string. When a pedal note appears in the upper voice of a chord or chord sequence it is referred to as an *'inverted pedal note'*. A pedal note is usually the dominant (5th) or tonic (root) of a chord though other intervals may be used. This device is not limited to jazz and has in fact been used by classical composers since the Renaissance period.

Bach used pedals in his fugues to create tension, whilst later Romantic composers like Sibielius and Mahler used it to stablilize their harmony. In jazz Charles Mingus and Thelonious Monk made much use of it in their compositions.

1 PEDALS USING THE 2nd STRING

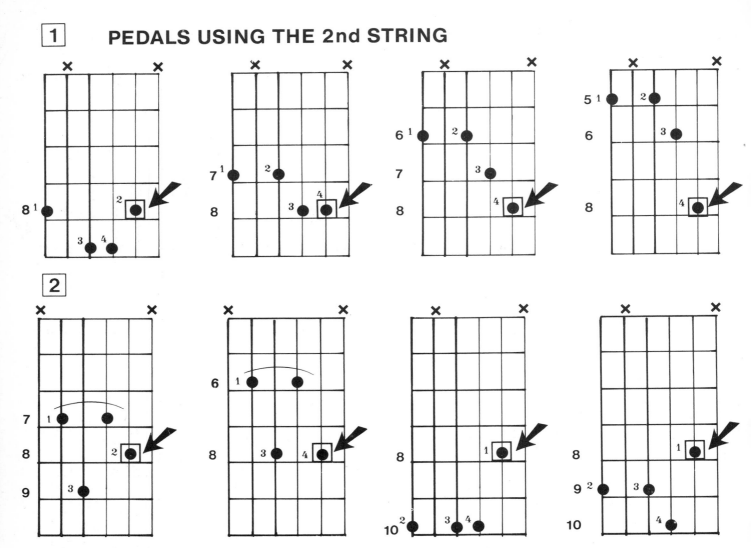

2

These sequences are very effective at the *'Turn-around'* point of a tune, which is usually at the verse end, where the tune progresses to the dominant chord and then begins all over again. They are also extremely tasteful used as an introduction, particularly to a slow ballad. They may also be used as chord connections, No. 1 can connect C (I) to Am7 VI7) and C (I) to Dmi7 (IIm7) and sequence No. 2 can be used to connect G (V) to C (I) and G (V) to Cm7 (Im7).

These chord sequences may also be employed when a G note is reiterated and a good example of this is Antonio Carlos Jobin's tune 'One Note Samba' which in fact used the second sequence shown here.

The fundamental uses of these pedals may be summarized as follows:

1. **over a repeated melody note (G).**

2. **over a repeated dominant chord.**

3. **over a repeated tonic chord.**

4. **in place of a dominant to tonic (turn around).**

5. **as an introduction.**

6. **as an ending.**

7. **as a device to connect chords together.**

PEDALS ON THE 1st STRING

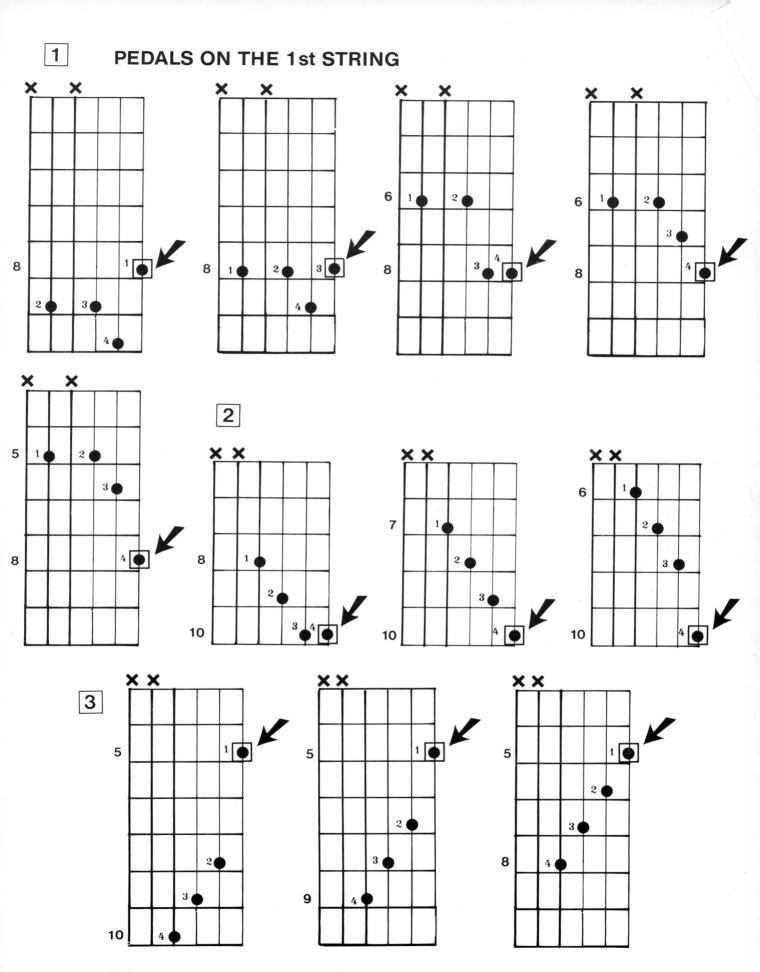

This sequence involves quite a large stretch between the first and second fingers and it takes most people a long time to master, so don't give up if you cannot do it at the first attempt!

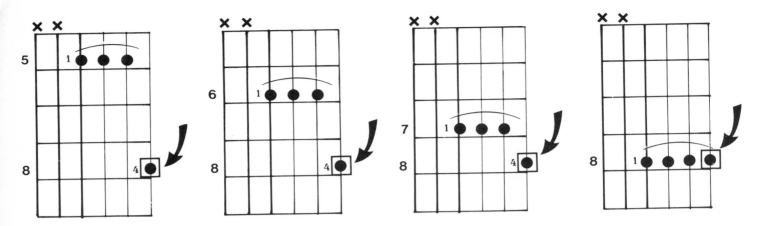

4 PEDALS USING THE 1st STRING

This progression is very effective when used in place of the major chord shape:

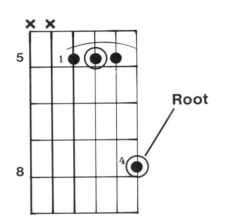

Root

The sustained root (4th finger 1st string) retains the feeling of the major chord and therefore the progression is restricted to the major key of the same name as the root note.

(C major)

PEDALS USING THE 6th STRING

The sustained note here is in the bass part, it is the Key note (tonic of C major) over which the chords descend chromatically between Cmi7 and C major chords. Jazz guitarists utilizing progressions with pedals in the bass usually employ syncopation, playing the pedal note slightly before the rest of the chord and effectively drawing attention to the bass note.

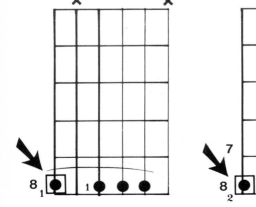
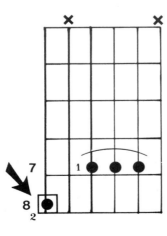
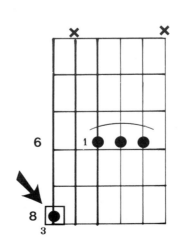
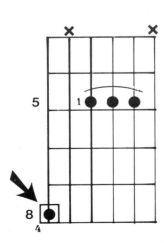

As with most other progressions using a pedal note this sequence can be substituted for any of the following:

1. **A sustained major chord.**

2. **A tonic to sub-dominant chord connection.**

3. **An introduction or an ending.**

4. **Over a chromatic melodic line descending between any of the following notes:**

G — E
E♭ — C
B♭ — G

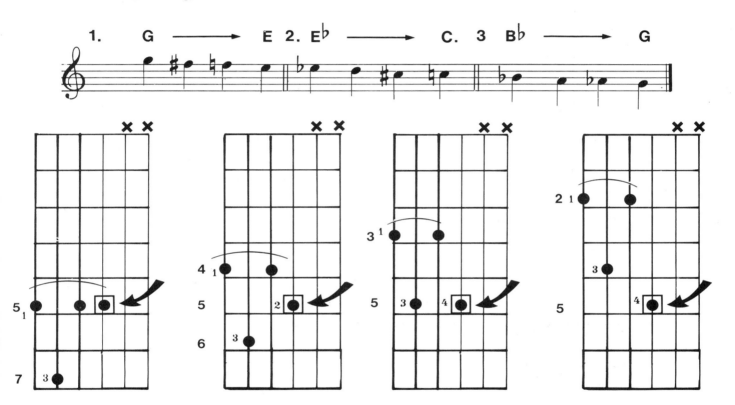

This beautiful progression is voiced in the bass, over a pedal on the 3rd string. It connects the Tonic (C) or submediant (Am or Ami7) to the subdominant (F) very well but because of it's bass voicing and the resulting low pitch, it is not suitable when playing with another harmonic instrument (i.e. piano, organ etc.).

RIFFING

There is a need for chord substitution when the same chord is reiterated over and over again, to relieve the monotony while other musicians are soloing.

We have already seen some of the things that are possible for example, minor thirds, altered chords, pedals and moving bass lines. It is also possible to create excitement and to drive the soloist along by constantly repeating a certain note or phase. The Count Basie band used this device a good deal behind its various soloists and so did Charles Mingus with his various groups in the late fifties and early sixties. Most jazz guitarists have also used the device at one time or another, particularly George Benson and Wes Montgomery.

Jazz musicians call it riffing but the 'official' term used in classical music for a repeated note or phrase that is sustained for any length of time is 'ostinato'.

The riff, or ostinato, is not restricted to a single line melody and can be made up from chords, octaves, and various intervals for example 3rds and 4ths and 5ths etc., a good way to begin riffing is with octaves as this can sound very effective. Even the use of one note and it's octave, providing that it is used thythmically can be successfully substituted for chords.

First choose your note, initially from within the basic chord i.e., G Chord — G B D and the Gm Chord — G B♭ D, and add the octave of that note. In general octaves on strings 1 to 4 sound the most effective as they have more bite.

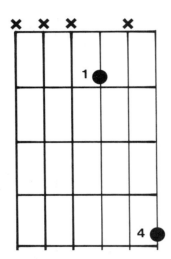 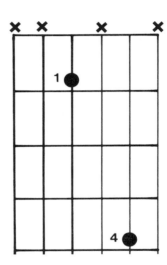

Invent your own rhythms making a mental note of the ones that work best so that you can use them again at a later date. Experiment also with notes from within the scales that relate to the chord, remembering that pentatonic and whole tone scales can be used, along with a major chord while both melodic and harmonic scales along with the various modes can be exploited for use over a minor chord*.

Above all listen hard to yourself and to those you are accompanying. Listen to the track "Paraphernalia" on the Miles Davies record 'Miles In The Sky' C.B.S. 63352 to hear how effective George Benson's hypnotic use of the octave (D) substitutes for a fuller chord.

Another record on which you will hear much of this technique is 'The Small Group Recordings' by Wes Montgomery, Verve double 2632 064, particularly in the opening blues.

*The chapter on related scales and modes from the theoretical section of this book should be used for reference.

To conclude this section on chords, here are two progressions for you to practice. Both of these progressions were used widely in the be-bop era (approx. 1944-54) and to this day they remain favourite vehicles for jazz improvisation, particularly during impromptu jam sessions.

1. BLUES IN B♭

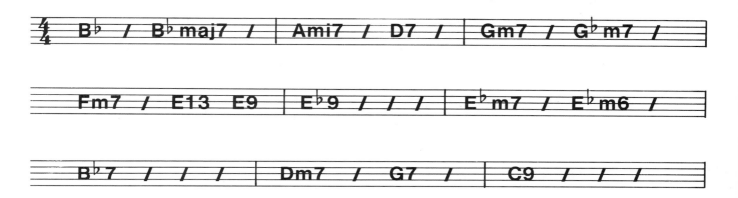

2. BE-BOP PROGRESSION

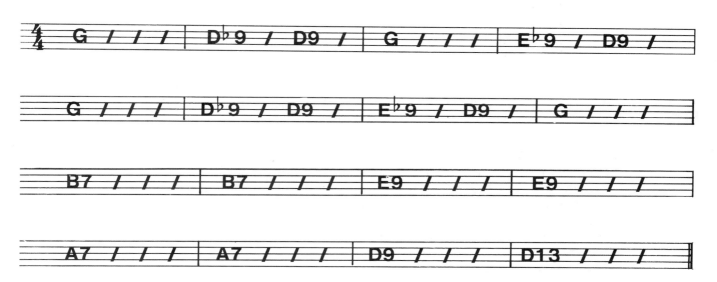

Try to memorize these two progressions, as they will prove most useful when you feel ready to jam with other musicians. It would also be a good idea for you to familiarize yourself with as many 'Standard' tunes as possible for these form the basis of a jazz guitarists literature. Many so-called jazz originals are in fact based on the chord changes of many such 'Standard' tunes for example, 'Anthropology', 'Oleo' and 'Salt Peanuts' are all based on 'I've Got Rhythm', 'Donna Lee' on 'Indiana' and 'Ornithology' on 'How High the Moon'.

WHAT NEXT?

In a book of this length it is impossible to go further into the study of jazz chords and their application.

If you have made it this far you have laid the foundations for a more 'in depth' study of the art form and contrary to what many players think, chord playing is an art in itself and many entire books have been devoted to the subject.

No single book or tutor in itself will make you a complete guitarist for there is always something new to learn, a new chord shape, a new combination of familiar ones, a new concept formed by a new young player who through his highly individual style makes the rest of us re-think our approach. The guitar and jazz music are both constantly evolving and as I have stressed many times in this book, you must always open your ears, *'listen and learn'* and hopefully you will become receptive to new ideas and new sounds so that the unfamiliar soon becomes the familiar, and the *'weird'* becomes the *'conventional'*.

If you feel that the art of chord playing is your particular forte, or if you feel that my relatively short introduction to the subject has given you the motivation to study the subject to a greater depth I can highly recommend the following texts:

Modern Chord Progressions, *Ted Greene.*
Chord Chemistry, (Dale Zdenek Publications).
The Complete Chord Book for Guitar, *Sal Salvador* (Belwin Mills).
Guitar Method, *George Van Eps* (Plymouth Music Co.).
Original Guitar Solos, *George Van Eps* (Plymouth Music Co.).
Joe Pass Chord Solos, *Joe Pass* (Gwyn Publishing Co.).
Guitar Manual Chord Melody, *Howard Roberts* (Playback).

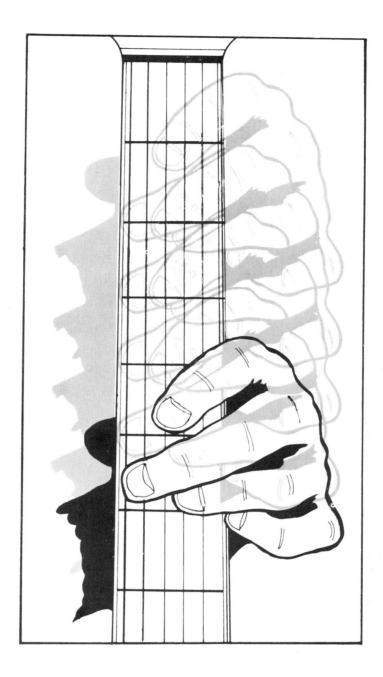

LINEAR
IMPROVISATION

SECTION THREE

LINEAR IMPROVISATION

The remainder of this book is concerned with single-string solo work. The basic principle behind what follows is that no matter who you choose to model yourself upon and no matter what style of jazz you wish to play, the most important first step is to thoroughly familiarize yourself with the instrument.

This book if used properly should provide you with a foundation for improvisation. Remember that you cannot hope to become a Wes Montgomery or George Benson overnight and that it takes many years of hard work to formulate an individual style.

The very nature of our instrument makes life difficult for we cannot execute incredibly rapid runs as easily as a saxophonist, as he can play these in one breath while we have to pick practically every note! We can also finger a phrase in two or more places, though when you are more familiar with the instrument this can be used to good advantage. The list could continue with our lack of sustaining power, the guitar's tendancy to encourage the use of habitual cliches, and so on and so forth.

Most Jazz guitar solos are based on what is fundamentally a saxophone style of long fluent streams of notes. As the saxophone has developed in jazz so too has the guitar, and comparisons may easily be made.

Charlie Christian had a similar approach to Lester Young, Tal Farlow and Jimmy Raney to Charlie Parker, John McLaughlin and Pat Martino to John Coltrane, Sonny Sharrok to Ornette Coleman and so on.

This continual development has broken down many of the old concepts and what is possible today was considered impossible a few years ago. Because of this continual rise in playing standards the jazz guitarist has to work harder than ever if he wishes to compete with the famous names in jazz.

What follows will start you off on the right tracks, giving you a basic knowledge of scale patterns and arpeggios, thus providing you with the most important tool of all 'Knowledge of your instrument'.

Almost every jazz solo derives from either a basic diatonic major or minor scale, the various modes, or newer scale patterns such as whole tone, blues, diminished and pentatonics, or a combination of these. Although a straight scale sounds too classical and doesn't give the required feeling in jazz:

The addition of dissonant notes such as the minor 7th of flattened 5th can bring a basic scale passage to life.

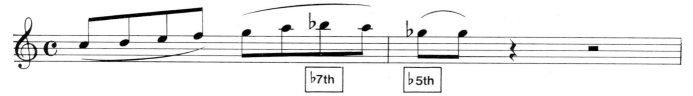

In jazz we are concerned with the transmission of ideas from the brain into sounds, from the instrument. To do this successfully requires **(a) sound technical facility, and (b) a complete knowledge of the fingerboard.**

Many jazz players do not read music but they know only too well what they are doing with the guitar. For by trial and error, listening to others and many years of experience these players have learnt the fingerboard extremely well and can play an idea instantaneously, usually with the ability to finger the same passage in at least two different places.

Unfortunately not every guitarist is blessed with an exceptionally good ear and therefore has to develop a systematic approach in order to acquire the necessary technical facility and knowledge of the fingerboard.

It is necessary to learn how to finger passages in different positions so that your own limitations do not hinder your creativity. If for example you heard this phrase in your mind.:

which continued something like this:

Then you would obviously have to finger it somewhere up the neck. If your knowledge as yet only enabled you to finger these notes in a lower position.

You would run into difficulties when trying to carry out your original intention of playing a higher pitched phrase immediately afterwards.

How then can we gain such familiarity with the fingerboard?

There seems to be two answers to this question, firstly if you have a very good ear you may gain this knowledge by trial and error, secondly, and this is the answer that the remainder of this book is based upon, you can acquire such knowledge by the use of systematic exercises including the time-honoured use of scales and arpeggios.

THE MAJOR SCALE

There are four basic fingerings for the major scale, each one relating to a major chord. These scales should therefore be used in connection with the chord shapes that are indicated. When constructing your own jazz solos always think in terms of the basic chord, for example think of G Major when you solo over G9, G13, G11, G7, G7♭5, etc. Then, use notes from the related major scales indicated below to construct your solo. By doing this you are building a sound foundation for all of your solo work, and additional notes such as 7ths, 9ths, 11ths and ♭5ths may be incorporated at a later date when you are more experienced in the use of basic scales.

(S)   **stands for which string to use.**

(F)   **stands for the fret to use.**

The fingering is indicated by figures accompanying each note, 1 for 1st finger, 2 for second, etc.

All of the following scale patterns may be moved up or down the fingerboard to form different scales. The examples below are all G Major scales.

1

| (S) | 6 | 6 | 5 | 5 | 5 | 4 | 4 | 4 | 3 | 3 | 3 | 2 | 2 | 1 | 1 |
| (F) | 3 | 5 | 2 | 3 | 5 | 2 | 4 | 5 | 2 | 4 | 5 | 3 | 5 | 2 | 3 |

This two octave scale form is by far the most useful because both octaves fall easily beneath the hand without the necessity of having to move out of the second position. The related chord shape of this pattern is:

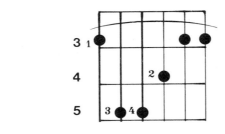

2

| (S) | 5 | 4 | 4 | 4 | 3 | 3 | 2 | 2 |
| (F) | 10 | 7 | 9 | 10 | 7 | 9 | 7 | 8 |

The related chord shape for this pattern is:

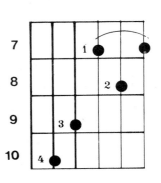

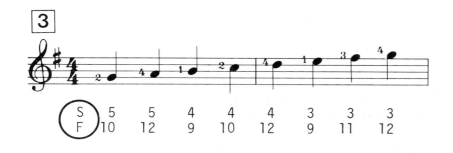

The related chord shape for this pattern is:

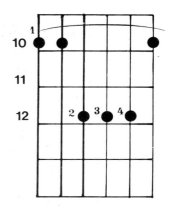

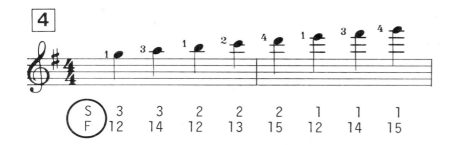

The related chord shape for this pattern is:

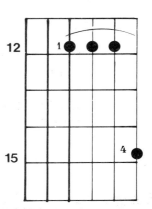

MAJOR SCALE EXTENSIONS

As most of these scale patterns are one octave only, it is possible to add extra notes from a lower or higher octave of the same scale, thereby giving a greater choice of notes for your solos.

To the first pattern we could add an F♯ below the first G and an A above the top one:

The 2nd, 3rd and 4th scale patterns offer much greater possibilities.

	S	6	6	5	5	5	4	4	4	3	3	3	2	2	1	1	1
	F	10	12	9	10	12	9	11	12	9	11	12	10	12	13	10	12

To extend this scale pattern needs a slight adjustment of the hand in the last bar (B to C) this involves sliding the fourth finger up a fret and effectively changing the position. This change of position can however be used to your advantage, giving you ready access to the fourth scale pattern and therefore the additional use of notes in your solo that are higher.

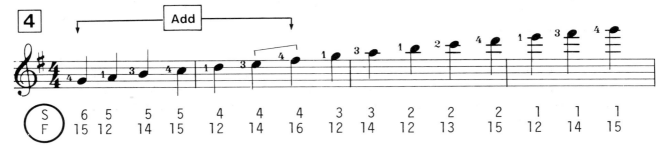

	S	6	5	5	5	4	4	4	3	3	2	2	2	1	1	1
	F	15	12	14	15	12	14	16	12	14	12	13	15	12	14	15

The only problem here is the stretch between the 3rd and 4th fingers in the second bar (indicated ⌐￢). However, this can be mastered quickly as stretches so high up the fingerboard are relatively small in distance.

PRACTICE PROCEDURE

Practice the four scale patterns with and without extensions until they are fluent. You must memorize them and practice them in connection with the related chords, moving them into new keys as soon as G Major has been thoroughly mastered.

If you really want to become a good soloist you must know these patterns backwards!

Try practicing them also by starting on a different note each time, e.g.

Now invent your own patterns by varying the order of the notes and changing the rhythms.

Although position playing with the use of these four scale patterns is an excellent way to learn the guitar fingerboard it can of course have its restrictions in that any form of pattern playing can inhibit creativity.

However, it is a step that must be taken in familiarizing yourself with the fingerboard. The next step is to join these scales together fluently so that it is possible to play three octaves.

The following three octave G major scale is again a finger pattern that can be moved into different keys, but one which is less restricting as you are increasing the range of notes that may be played against a chord.

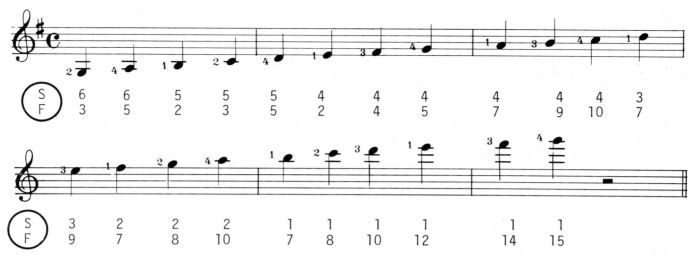

SCALE RUNS

All of these scale patterns are formed from a G Major scale and, once memorized, should be moved into other keys. Where practical each run is given three times (a.b. and c) in a different octave so that they can be played in different places on the fingerboard.

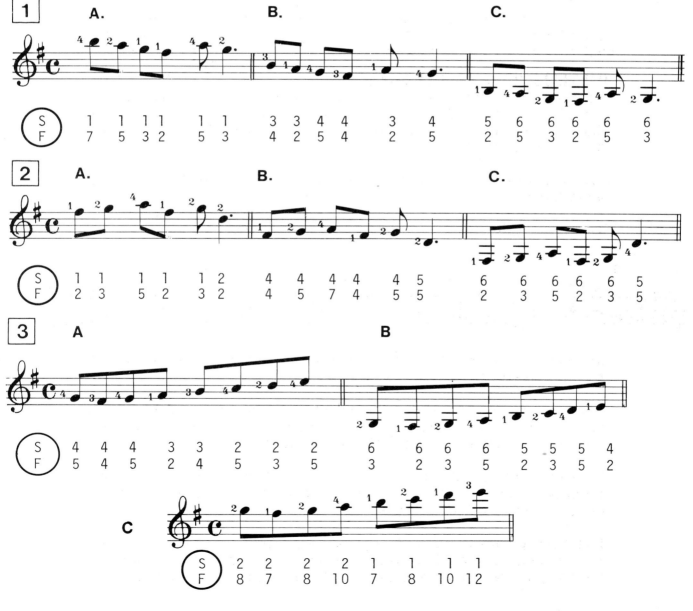

B

C Alternative fingering in the VII position.

9

It is also possible to form a run on each degree of the scale.

I   II

III   IV

V   VI

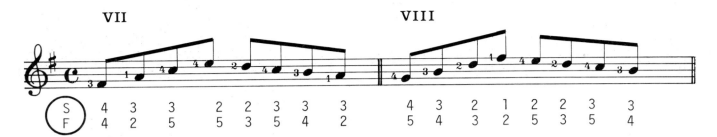

Invent your own scale runs using the various G scale patterns and remember that you do not necessarily have to begin or end with the note G.

SCALE RUNS WITH AN ADDED ♭7th NOTE

The additional use of passing notes such as the ♭7th (minor 7th) ♭5th, 9th and ♯5th gives a better jazz feel.

The addition of the ♭7th note is the most popular.

The 7th note of the scale is flattened (in this case made into a natural) giving us an extra note, the ♭7 (or minor 7th) which is so common that it is usually referred to as the 7th.

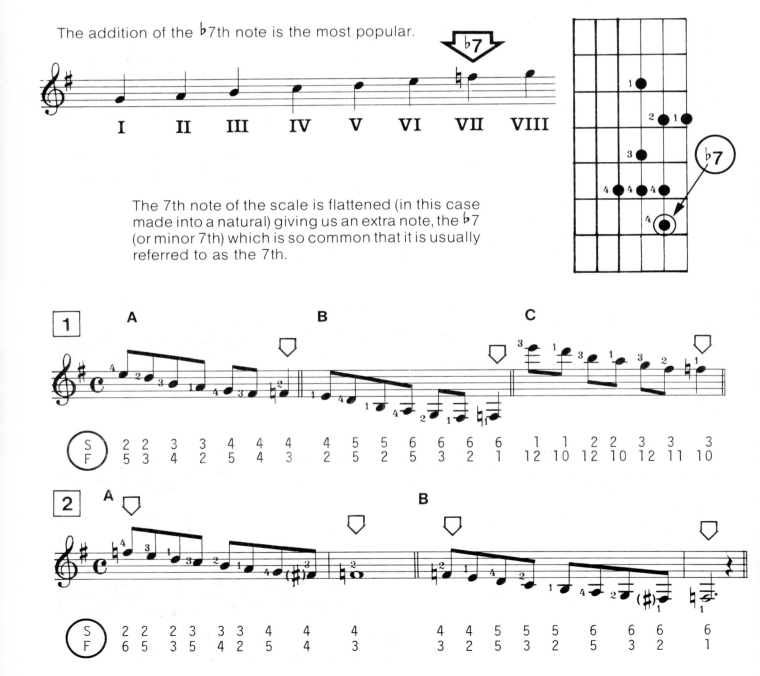

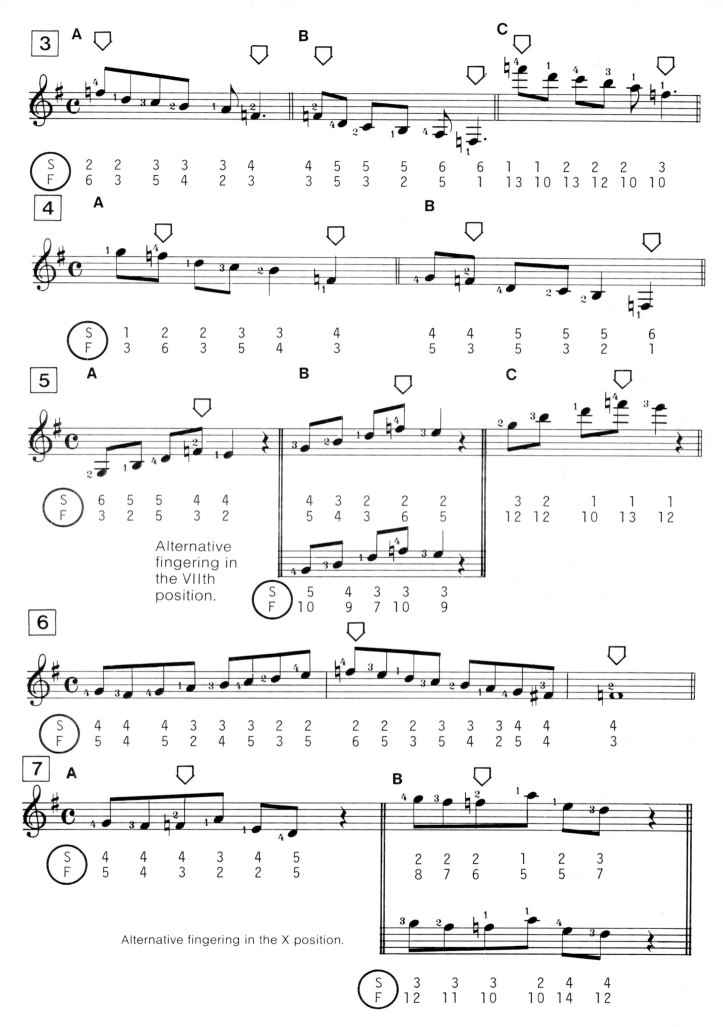

Scale runs with the added 7th are particularly good for connecting tonic and sub-dominant chords. The 7th note when lowered a semitone (one fret) becomes an essential note (a 3rd) of the sub-dominant chord.

Try connecting the following chords with scale runs, dropping the 7th note one fret to become a note of the new chord.

A Major

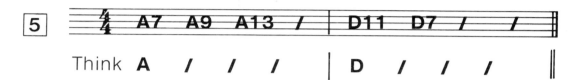

SCALE RUNS USING FLATTENED FIFTHS (♭5th)

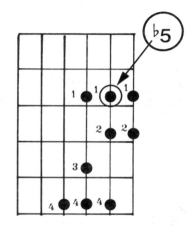

The ♭5th is also widely used in jazz, practice the following runs and then try inventing some of your own.

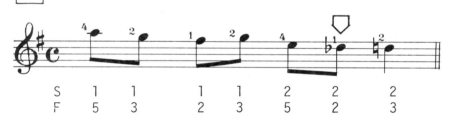

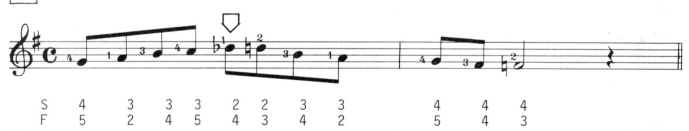

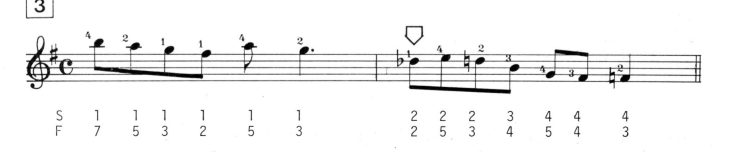

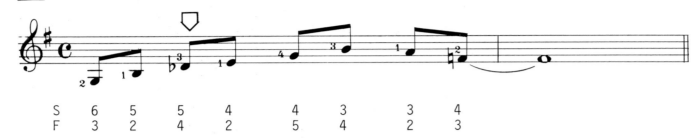

S	6	5	5	4	4	3	3	4
F	3	2	4	2	5	4	2	3

5

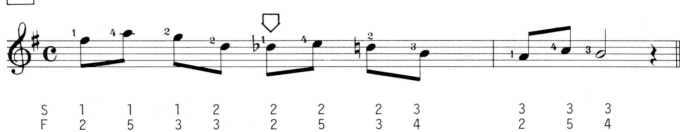

S	1	1	1	2	2	2	2	3	3	3	3
F	2	5	3	3	2	5	3	4	2	5	4

THE MINOR SCALE

There are two different minor scales, the harmonic which has it's 7th note sharpened,

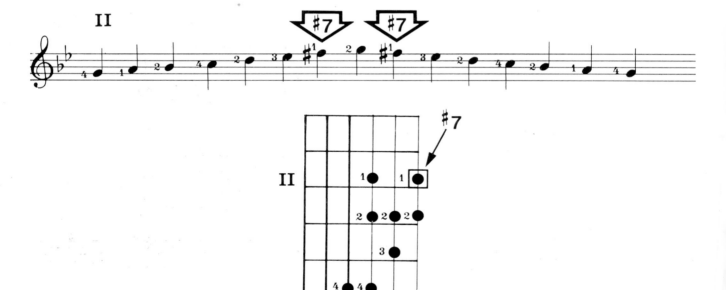

and the melodic, which has its 6th and 7th note sharpened ascending and restored descending.

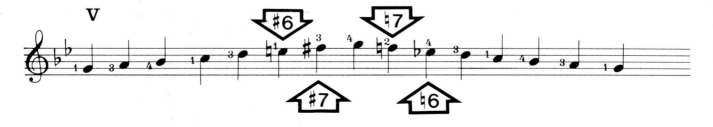

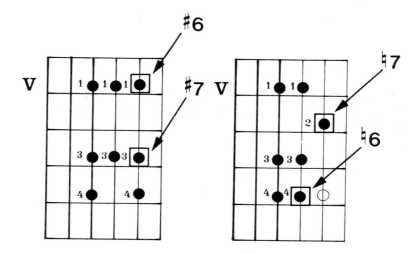

For jazz purposes the harmonic minor scale is the most widely used though players often use a combination of both harmonic and melodic minors in their improvision.

As with the major scale there are four basic finger patterns each of which relates to a particular chord shape. The harmonic minor scales below are all in G minor.

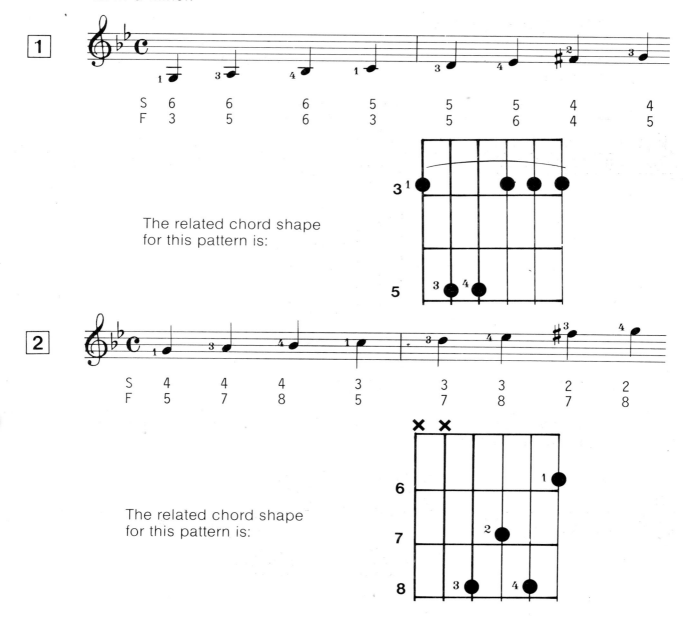

The related chord shape for this pattern is:

The related chord shape for this pattern is:

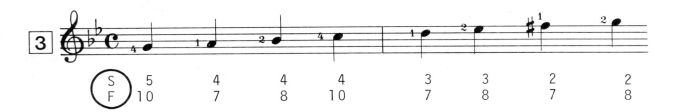

3

S/F	5/10	4/7	4/8	4/10	3/7	3/8	2/7	2/8

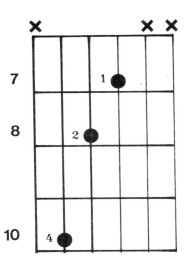

The related chord shape for this pattern is:

4

S/F	5/10	5/12	5/13	4/10	4/12	4/13	3/11	3/12

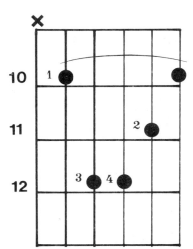

The related chord shape for this pattern is:

MINOR SCALE EXTENSIONS

1

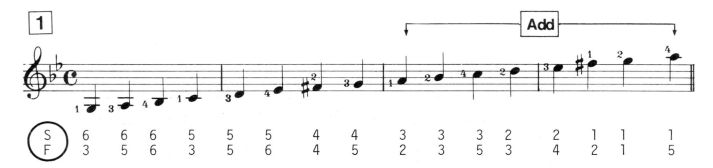

S/F	6/3	6/5	6/6	5/3	5/5	5/6	4/4	4/5	3/2	3/3	3/5	2/3	2/4	1/2	1/1	1/5

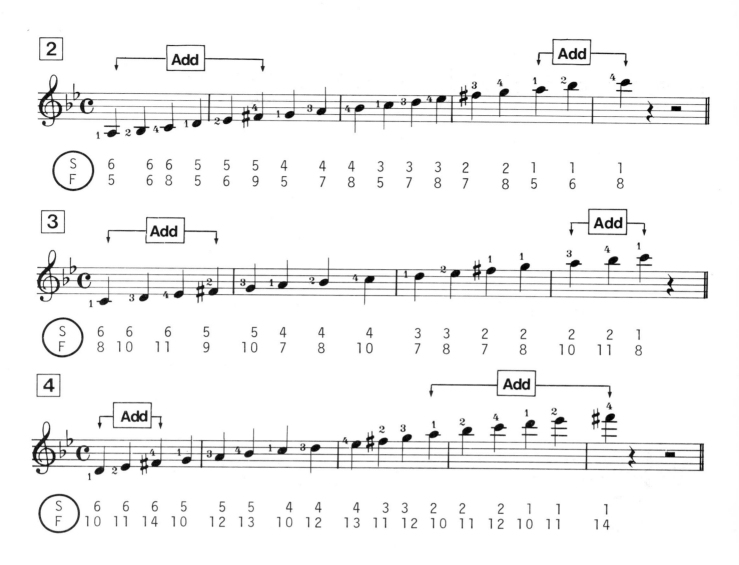

MINOR SCALE RUNS

Runs using a combination of harmonic and melodic minor notes.

with a ♭5th

BLUE NOTES

Blue notes are extra notes added to a major scale which give it a distinctive jazz sound.

These notes are found by lowering the 3rd, the 5th and the 7th degrees one semitone (a fret).

It is common to find these lowered notes side by side with the unaltered ones:

You will find that this scale is sometimes referred to as the *'jazz scale'*.

Blue notes are thought to be the result of an integration of negro and white cultures sometime during the early period of negro slavery in the USA. These notes came into general use because the combination of the negro pentatonic (5 note) scale and the European diatonic (8 note) scale led to difficulties of pitch for the negro, they preferred to flatten the 3rd and the 7th, the ♭5 was a much later development.

The success of the blue note depends largely on its tonal ambiguity, for example the inclusion of both the ♭3rd and the 3rd in the same phrase results in a curious blend of major and minor tonality.

Below are some major scale runs including the ♭3rd (minor 3rd). The ♭5 and ♭7 have already been met earlier on as passing notes.

MAJOR SCALE RUNS USING FLATTENED THIRDS (♭3rd)

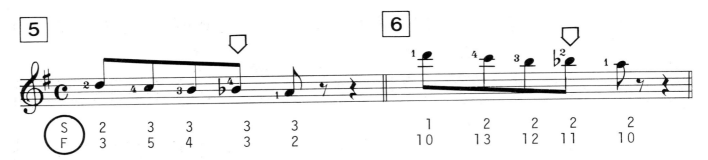

IMPROVISING OVER A CHORD SEQUENCE

Now that you have a few ideas for soloing over a single chord the next step is to improvise over a progression of chords. This involves the connection of one scale run to another. Except in a few isolated cases a scale or scale run will contain at least one note from the related scale of the following chord.

C Related Scale

If for example you were soloing over a C chord and using the above notes, any of these could be thought of as the Keynote (root) of the next chord. By adopting this method a C chord could lead naturally on to the chords and related scales of D, E, F, G, A and B both majors and minors.

The result is that any note from the related scale of C may be used as the starting note of a different related scale.

With careful planning you can create scale runs that end with a note which begins the related scale of the following chord.

This sequence uses the related scale of each chord* (basic chord not 9ths etc.) each of which is connected smoothly by treating certain notes as if they belong to two related scales instead of one. In the first bar the A of the C scale is also the root (1st note) of the Am scale thus leading us smoothly into the bar of Ami7. In the second bar the F of the Am harmonic scale is treated as the root of the F scale and in the 3rd bar the E note from the F scale is treated as the root of an E scale.

*Always reduce your chords to their bare tonality when improvising i.e., M9, Mi6, Mi7 became ordinary minors, 7ths, 9th, 11th ♭5ths become ordinary majors.

Other notes of the related scale may also be used as connections providing that they appear somewhere in the related scale of the following chord.

Here is an example in G major the connecting notes common to both chords are marked*.

Try improvising over the following chords using related scales and scale connections.

| F / / / | Fmaj7 / / / | Emi7 / / / | A7 / / / |

| Dmi / / / | G7 / / / | Cmi7 / / / | F7 / / / |

| B♭maj7 / / / | B♭mi7 / / / | F7 / / / | Dmi7 / / / |

| Gmi7 / / / | C9 / / / | F7 / / / | C9 / / / |

THE DIMINISHED SCALE

Diminished and Augmented chords pose more problems than majors or minors. Such chords are generally used only in passing and are seldom sustained for any length of time.

A diminished chord can take its name from any of the notes within it for example a Cdim chord is also an E♭dim, an F♯dim or an Adim.

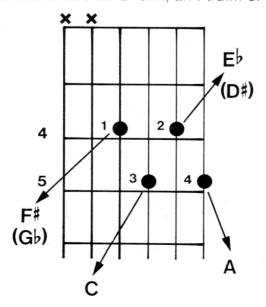

Because of this peculiarity there are basically only three diminished chords, C, C♯ and D, every other diminished chord being an inversion of one of these.

Cdim is also **E♭ dim, F♯ dim, Adim.**

C♯dim is also **Edim, Gdim, B♭ dim.**

D dim is also **Fdim, A♭ dim, B♭ dim.**

There are also three diminished scales each one relating to the three basic chords. By memorizing these you will be able to improvise over any of the twelve diminished chords listed above.

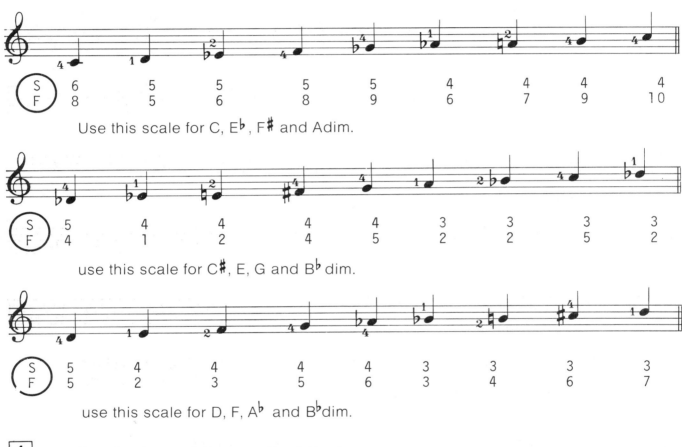

Use this scale for C, E♭, F♯ and Adim.

use this scale for C♯, E, G and B♭ dim.

use this scale for D, F, A♭ and B♭dim.

1   Practice improvising over the following sequences:

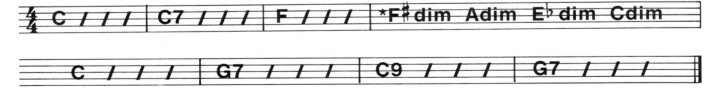

*Although this bar looks very hard to improvise over, it is basically three inversions of the same (Cdim) chord, and it is possible to use the same scale for the entire bar, e.g.

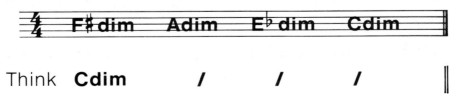

Think   **Cdim**   /   /   /   ‖

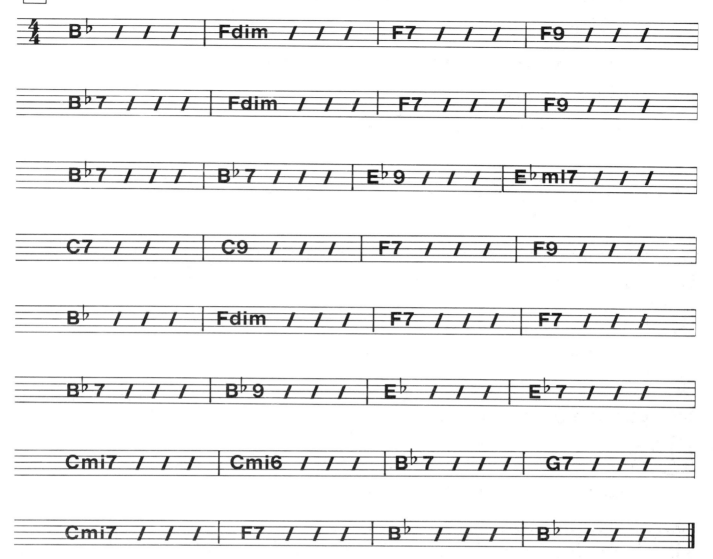

2

This sequence is based on a blues by Jelly Roll Morton. The diminished chords in bars two and six are used only in passing and their use here typifies the role of a diminished chord.

THE AUGMENTED SCALE (WHOLE TONE)

This scale is constructed from intervals a tone (two frets) apart and is referred to by most as the 'whole tone' scale. It gives a vague feeling, for no one note seems to be the key note. This scale's lack of a definable key centre makes it particularly suitable to use against an augmented chord which, like the diminished chord, also has four possible key notes.

There are two whole tone scales, C and C♯ these can be used for all augmented chords.

C Whole Tone Scale is used against Caug, Daug, Eaug, F♯aug, A♭aug and B♭aug.

C♯ Whole Tone Scale is used against C♯aug, E♭aug, Faug, Gaug, Aaug and Baug.

1. C Whole Tone Scale

S	5	5	5	4	4	4	3	3	3	2	2	2	1
F	3	5	7	4	6	8	5	7	9	7	9	11	8

use this scale for C, D, E, F, A and B♭ augmented.

2. C♯ Whole Tone Scale

S	5	5	5	4	4	4	3	3	3	2	2	2	1
F	4	6	8	5	7	9	6	8	10	8	10	12	9

use this scale for C♯, E♭, F, G, A, and B augmented.

Improvise over the following chord sequence using the whole tone scale for C♯ for the Gaug bar and the scale of C for F♯aug.

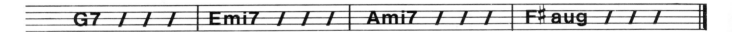

OCTAVES

The use of octaves (the doubling of a unison note at a higher or lower pitch) is very popular with jazz guitarists. Although both Django Reinhardt and Teddy Bunn used octaves in their improvisations many years earlier it was Wes Montgomery who popularised the technique in the 1960's.

There are many ways to finger octaves with the left hand but the ones used most frequently are those listed below. The reason for this is that these shapes leave only one string in between to dampen whereas other fingerings would leave two.

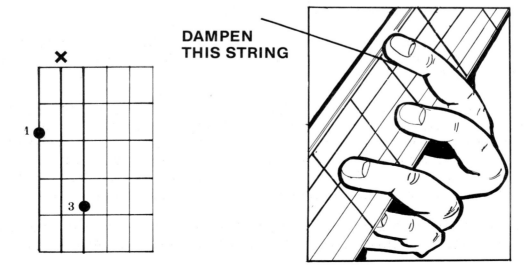

DAMPEN THIS STRING

110

The 6th string shape which is moveable, is transferred over to the 5th string to form an octave between strings 5 and 3.

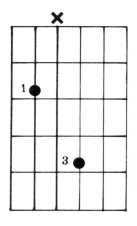
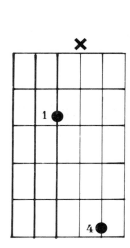

The 4th and 3rd string octave shapes use a different fingering, which is also used for the 3rd and 1st string octave shape.

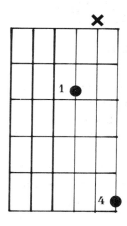

String damping in octave playing

When you play octaves you obviously only want the two fingered strings to sound, and this involves the technique of damping (or deadening) the string that falls between.

To achieve this it is necessary to flatten the first joint of your first finger, just enough to make contact with the adjacent string. It is important that contact is only just made and that you don't use too much pressure, otherwise the offending string will sound! If you are using a pick use all down strokes. Wes Montgomery obtained his beautiful tone through the use of the right hand thumb, not only on octaves, but also for every fast single string runs.

As mentioned earlier in the section on riffing, octaves may be used in place of a chord. Try using octaves in this way before attempting any solo work.

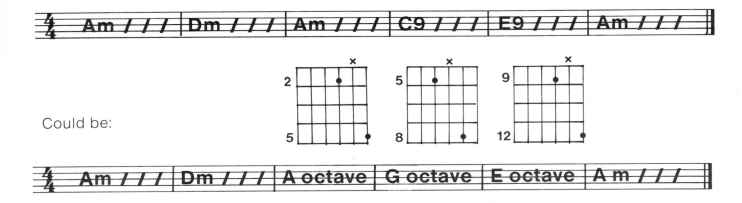

Could be:

The following tune will give you more practice in the use of octaves. It can be played entirely with the 4th and 2nd string octave shape, and the 3rd and 1st string octave shape:

WES

A. Ingram

MELODIC IMPROVISATION

Most of the work in this book has been concerned with harmonic improvisation, that is improvisation based on chord changes, for this style has been the norm since the late 40's.

However, earlier jazz musicians played in a different style, the style of melodic embellishment, that is the ornamentation in varying degrees of the original tune. Early musicians thought of jazz as an embellishment of the melody and that the actual melody should never be far from the surface. The jazz academic Gunther Schuller* calls this "referential improvisation" whilst in modern day practice it is called "theme" paraphrase. Louis Armstrong was the great master of the style although in the strict sense his style was also harmonic, for he was far more adventurous than his contemporaries, sometimes wandering far away from the original tune.

Many of the devices used for melodic improvisation have now become common place and deserve a brief mention.

1. Sub Division

Breaking a note into others of a shorter value, for example two quavers ♫ for a crotchet ♩ or two semi quavers ♬ for a quaver. This device is called "diminution" by classical musicians.

2. Neighbour Notes

The melody note is preceded by a note one or two frets above or below it;

Melody Notes

With Neighbour notes

3. Passing Notes

Connecting melody notes with scale notes either diatonic or chromatic;

Melody

With passing notes

Passing notes are particulary effective when the melody notes are separated by an interval of a 4th or more;

Melody

With passing notes

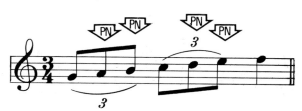

4. Retardation

Playing the melody note later than usual;

Melody

With retarded melody

(*"Early Jazz", Oxford University Press, 1968.)

5. Anticipation

The opposite to retardation, playing the melody note before its actual time.

Melody

with anticipated melody

BE-BOP BLUES

PLAYING OUTSIDE

Playing outside or side-slipping is a term used by jazz musicians for a given key, chord or chord progression. An alien key or chord that contrasts sharply with the original one is used by the soloist whilst at least one member of the group continues to play the original chord or chord progression.

This device is not unlike the use of pedals discussed earlier, where a single note is retained whilst chords move freely and chromatically against it.

Playing outside is particularly effective in a modal tune where the repetition of an anchoring bass line gives a beautiful effect of dramatic tension, the end result being closely akin to bi-tonality (the sounding of two keys simultaneously). However it can also sound as if a new section has been added to the original chord sequence or as if the player is deliberately playing 'wrong notes'.

Jazz players use this device a good deal, perhaps the most famous example occurs in the tune 'A Love Supreme' by John Coltrane (Impulse 8001). Most of Coltrane's work is worthy of study and the later works particularly are full of these side-slips. Of the Guitar players, both Pat Martino an George Benson favour this device.

Playing outside generally has some of the following characteristics:—

(1) The new key will be in total opposition to the old one (outside of it).

(2) A musical phrase used in the original key is repeated immediately in the new key, often several times in succession to reinforce the change.

(3) The player quickly returns to the original key, though some highly skilled players continue to drift through several different unrelated keys.

The following example illustrates the use of the side-slip in bars 4, 7 and 9, where the soloist plays a semitone (one fret) higher than his accompaniment.

SUITE FOR THREE GUITARS (extract)

A. Ingram

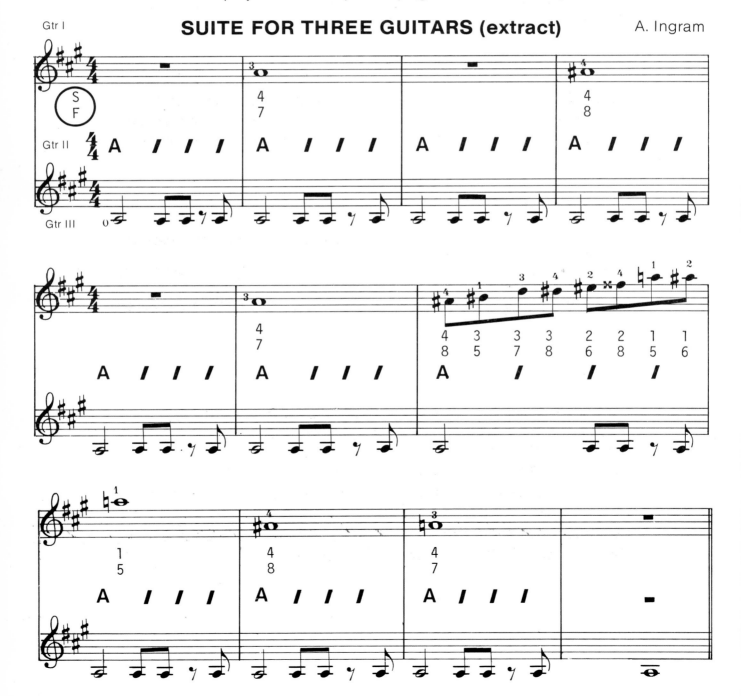

FURTHER STUDY

The major, minor, diminished and augmented scales that you have just learnt are some of the resources for linear improvisation. Draw on these for your improvisations and when you feel that they are restricting, in other words when your own ideas are such that they cannot be conveyed with these devices, pursue the related scale technique further.

You can do this by learning new scales such as the pentatonic or chromatic and all of the modes which are mentioned briefly in the theoretical section of this book. A list of books follows and many of these will prove useful in following up the work in this book.

In the meantime learn as many chord sequences as possible and then practice improvising over them. All of the great jazz soloists use habitual note patterns to some extent so don't be alarmed if at first you find you are repeating yourself, for this should change as you listen to more jazz and gradually become receptive to new ideas.

Recommended magazines including many that regularly feature articles on jazz guitar, jazz guitar players and other interesting topics on modern jazz.

Guitar Magazines

Fretwire, Fretwire Enterprises, 103 Nicholson Avenue, Macclesfield, Cheshire. Telephone: 20102 (0625)
Guitar, Musical New Services Ltd., 20 Denmark Street, London, WC2 8NE. Telephone: 01-836 2325
Guitar Player, GPI Publications, Box 615 (12333 Saratoga/Sunnyvale Road), Saratoga, C.A., U.S.A.

General

Black Music and Jazz Review, 1 Throwley Way, Sutton, Surrey.
Beat Instrumental, 16 Parkfield Street, London N1 0PR.
Crescendo, 122 Wardour Street, London W1.
Downbeat, 222 W. Adams Street, Chicago II-60606, U.S.A.
International Musician, Cover Publications Ltd., Grosvenor House, 141-143 Drury Lane, London WC2.
Jazz Journal, Pitman Periodicals Ltd., 39 Parker Street, London.
Melody Maker, 1 Throwley Way, Sutton, Surrey.

Recommended Reading

Harmony and jazz theory

Patterns for Improvisation, *Oliver Nelson.*
Thesaurus of Scales and Melodic Patterns, *N. Slonimsky.*
New Concepts in Linear Improvisation, *R. Rilker.*
The Professional Arranger and Composer, *R. Garcia.*
Jazz Improvisation, *D. Baker.*
All are published by Jamey Aubersold, New Albany, U.S.A.
Jazz – An Introduction to its Musical Basis, *A. Dankworth O.U.P.*
Popular and Jazz Harmony, *Rieigliano* (Donalto).

Improvisation

The Lydian Chromatic Concept of Tonal Improvisation, *George Russell*
(Concept Publications).
Improvising Jazz, *Jerry Coker* (Prentice Hall).
Jazz, *Graham Collier* (Cambridge University Press).
Jazz Improvisation, *John Mehagan* (Chappells).

General

The Jazz Guitar, *Maurice Summerfield* (Ashley Mark).
Interviews with jazz Guitarists, Guitar Player Publications.
Charlie Christian Guitar Solos, *Jamey Aebersold.*
Intervallic Designs, *Joe Diorio* (R.E.H. Publications).
Jazz Guitar Masterpieces, *Rich Carter* (Flat Five Publishing Co.).
World's Greatest Jazz Solos, *Mundell Lowe* (Almo Publications).
Jazz Is, *Nat Hentoff* (W. H. Allen).
Single String Studies for Guitar, *Sal Salvador* (Belwin Mills).
Jazz – A History, *Frank Tirro* (Dent & Sons).
Harmony for Guitar, *Lance Bosman* (Musical New Services).
The Guitar Player Book, (Guitar Player Publications).
The Artistry of John Coltrane, *Don Sickler/Bobby Porcelli* (Big 3 Music).
The Charlie Parker Omnibook (Transcriptions), (Atlantic Music Corp.).
Wes Montgomery Jazz Guitar Solos, *Fred Sokolow* (Almo Publications).
Jazz Styles, *Mark Grindley* (Prentice-Hall).

CHORDS

Solo Chords, *Roger Hutchinson* (R.E.H.).
Chord Confidence, *Roger Hutchinson* (R.E.H.).

Also see the article "What Next" on page **86** of this book, and the Author's
series on Chord Substitution in "Guitar Magazine", 1977-78.

RECOMMENDED LISTENING

GUITAR RECORDS

It's Uptown, *George Benson* (CBS 62817).
Benson's Cookbook, *George Benson* (CBS 62971).
White Rabbit, *George Benson* (CTI 6015).
Blue Benson, *George Benson* (Polydor 2391-242 Pol 320).
5 O'Clock Bells, *Lenny Breau* (Adelphi AD 5006).
Minors Aloud, *Lenny Breau and Buddy Emmons* (Sonet SNTF 799).
Alone Together, *Dennis Budimir* (Rev. 1).
A Second Coming, *Dennis Budimir* (Rev. 4).
Kenny Burrel/John Coltrane, *Kenny Burrel* (Prestige P24059).
Guitar Forms, *Kenny Burrel* (Verve VLP 9099).
Tin Tin Deo *(Kenny Burrel)* Concord CJ 45).
Twin House, *P. Catherine/L. Coryell* (Atlantic 50342).
Solo Flight *Charlie Christian* (CBS 67233).
Soft and Mellow, *Herb Ellis* (Concord CJ77).
The Red Norvo Trio (Double), *Tal Farlow* (Savoy 2212 0798).
The Red Norvo Trio, *Tal Farlow* (Natural Organic 7001).
Early Tal, *Tal Farlow* (Bluenote BNP 25104).
Autumn in New York, *Tal Farlow* (Norgan 1097).
The Fuerst Set, *Tal Farlow* (Xanadu 109).
The Second Set, *Tal Farlow* (Xanadu 119).
Trinity, *Tal Farlow* (CBS Sony 25AP 597).
Jazz Winds from a New Direction, *Hank Garland* (Columbia JCS 8372).
Jim Hall Live, *Jim Hall* (Horizon SP 705).
Alone Together, *Jim Hall* (Milestones MSP 9045).
The Jimmy Guiffre Three, *Jim Hall* (London LTL K 15130).
Jim Hall Trio, *Jim Hall* (Vogue LAE 12072).
The Pollwinners No. 1, *Barney Kessel* (Contemporary C3535).
Soaring, *Barney Kessel* (Concord CJ 33).
Kessel at Sometime, *Barney Kessel* (Trio PAP 9062).
Footprints, *Pat Martino* (Muse 5096).
Exit, *Part Martino* (Muse 5075).
We'll Be Together Again, *Pat Martino* (Muse 5090).
Consciousness, *Pat Martino* (Muse 5039).
Extrapolation, *John McLaughlin* (Polydor 231-018).
My Goal's Beyond, *John McLaughlin* (Douglas 220766).
The Trio, *Wes Montgomery* (Riverside 1156).
Boss Guitar, *Wes Montgomery* (Riverside 9459).
Moving Along, *Wes Montgomey* (Riverside 9342).
So Much Guitar, *Wes Montgomery* (Riverside 9382).
The Incredible Jazz Guitar of Wes Montgomery, *Wes Montgomery* (Riverside RLP 12320).
Full House, *Wes Montgomery* (Riverside RLP 9434).
Movin Wes, *Wes Montgomery* (Verve VLP 9092).
Catch Me, *Joe Pass* (Fontana 68813726).
For Django, *Joe Pass* (Fontana 6881462L).
2 For The Road, *Joe Pass* (Pablo 2310714).
Virtuoso, *Joe Pass* (Pablo 2310708).
Virtuoso, *Joe Pass* (Pablo 2310788).
Virtuoso, *Joe Pass* (Pablo 2310805).
Intercontinental, *Joe Pass* (MPS CRM 738).

The Influence, *Jimmy Raney* (Xanadu 116).
Live in Tokyo, *Jimmy Raney* (Xanadu 132).
Solo, *Jimmy Raney* (Xanadu 140).
The Real Howard Roberts, *Howard Roberts* (Concord CJ53).
Moonlight in Vermont, *Johnny Smith* (Roost YW & YW 810 RD).
Meeting Mr. Thomas, *Rene Thomas* (Blue Star 80708).
Interactions, *Chuck Wayne* (Choice CRS 1004).
Skyliner, *Chuck Wayne* (Progressive KUX 23G).

General Jazz Records

Giant Steps, *John Coltrane* (Atlantic 1311).
A Love Supreme, *John Coltrane* (IMPL 8001).
Blue Trane, *John Coltrane* (Blue Note BST 81577).
Black Pearls, *John Coltrane* (Prestige 24037).
More Lasting the Bronze, *John Coltrane* (Prestige 4014).
My Favourite Things, *John Coltrane* (Atlantic 128005).
Study in Brown, *Clifford Brown* (EmArcy 6336 708).
At Basin Street, *Clifford Brown* (EmArcy 6336 707).
Images, *The Crusaders* (ABC Records ABCL 5250).
Birth Of The Cool, *Miles Davies* (Capitol CAPS 1024).
Kind of Blue, *Miles Davies* (CB 62066).
Milestones, *Miles Davies* (PC 9428).
Miles In The Sky, *Miles Davies* (CBS 63352).
In A Silent Way, *Miles Davies* (CBS 63630).
Mingus Ah Um!, *Charlie Mingus* (CBS 52346).
Blues and Roots, *Charlie Mingus* (Atlantic 1305).
Mingus Dynasty, *Charlie Mingus* (CBS SCPG 62261).
Candid Recordings, *Charlie Mingus* (CBS 64675).
Monk/Coltrane, *Thelonius Monk* (Milestone M470 11).
Brilliance, *Thelonius Monk* (Milestone M47023).
Straight No Chaser, *Thelonius Monk* (CBS C5 9451).
Misterioso, *Thelonius Monk* (CBS CS 9216).
Presenting The Gerry Mulligan Sextet, (EmArcy 6336712).
East Broadway Rundown, *Sonny Rollins* (IMPL 8035).
Rollins, On Impulse, *Sonny Rollins* (IMP A 91).
Newk's Time, *Sonny Rollins* (Blue Note BST 84001).
Charlie Parker Rare Broadcasting Performances, *Charlie Parker* (Jazz Anthology 30JA 5164).
International Jam Sessions, *Charlie Parker* (Xanadu 1229).
Jazz at Massey Hall, *Charlie Parker* (Saga 8031).
The Amazing Bud Powell, *Bud Powell* (Blue Note BST 81503 and 81504).
Ezz-Thetics, *George Russel Sextet* (Riverside 9375).
Out To Lunch, *Eric Dolphy* (Blue Note BST 83163).
Heavy Weather, *Weather Report* (CBS 81775).

The above selection is by no means comprehensive, but should serve to give you an understanding of the development of jazz from the late forties to the present time.